D1553719

The
Enlightened
Gardener
Revisited

pg' 08

The Enlightened Gardener Revisited

A NOVEL BY

Sydney Banks

Lone Pine Publishing

The Publisher and Distributor: Lone Pine Publishing

10145 – 81 Avenue	1808 B Street NW, Suite 140
Edmonton, AB T6E 1W9	Auburn, WA, 98001
Canada	USA

Website: www.lonepinepublishing.com

Library and Archives Canada Cataloguing in Publication

Banks, Sydney
    The enlightened gardener revisited / Sydney Banks.

ISBN-13: 978-1-55105-158-1
ISBN-10: 1-55105-158-3

    I. Title.
PS8553.A57E543 2006   C813'.54   C2005-903988-4

Editorial Director: Nancy Foulds
Project Editor: Gary Whyte
Production Manager: Gene Longson
Book Design and Layout: Curt Pillipow, Heather Markham, Willa Kung
Cover Design: Gerry Dotto
Scanning, Separations & Film: Elite Lithographers Co.

We acknowledge the financial support of the Government of Canada through the Book Publishing Industry Development Program (BPIDP) for our publishing activities.

PC: P1

Table of Contents

A Note to the Reader

The story and characters portrayed in this book are fictional and simply a vehicle for expressing the author's philosophical beliefs. Through a series of conversations, the characters draw out an understanding of the essence of the Three Principles of Mind, Consciousness and Thought.

Chapter One
Returning to England

*O*n the twenty-third of June 1969, my associate, Dr. Janet Maxwell, and I boarded Flight 314 to London, the last leg of our journey to England. Once we were settled and comfortable, the plane's engines droning in the background, I found myself pondering the enormous changes that had occurred in both our lives. We were now experiencing a quality of happiness that neither of us could have imagined possible a short time ago. The transformation started two years ago when I first attended a psychology conference held close to the beautiful little village of Burton-on-the-Water. There, I had had the good fortune to meet an extraordinary English gardener by the name of Andy Miller. I was so taken by his philosophy that the following year I had urged some friends, including Janet, to accompany me to meet with him again. This simple gardener talked in such a mystical manner that we barely understood much of what he said. But whatever we did absorb gave us answers far beyond anything we could have imagined to questions raised during our professional training

He had talked about the world being a mystical, divine dream, saying that we are the dreamers; now Janet and I found all our dreams were coming true. The trouble is, neither of us understood why our lives were becoming better and better everyday, so now we were returning to spend more time with the mysterious gardener and examine more thoroughly his most unusual philosophy regarding the secret of the mind.

After an eight-hour flight, we were grateful to arrive at Heathrow Airport just outside London. We cleared Customs, then hailed a taxi to take us to the hotel where we were to stay the night. Tired as we were, it still felt wonderful to be back in England again and we were keyed up in anticipation of the adventure of discovery we were about to begin.

The following morning after breakfast, we headed to Waterloo Railway Station full of excitement at the thought of meeting the mysterious gardener again. We boarded a train crowded with all kinds of people; businessmen and women in somber suits sat next to youthful travelers in brightly colored and wildly original outfits, elderly couples on day trips smiled serenely at young families enjoying a holiday atmosphere. Mothers who appeared to have their hands full tried, with some success, to keep exuberant children in their seats. Fifteen minutes later, the train pulled out of the station and we were on our way to Torquay, where the gardener now resided. Janet and I admired the beauty of the English countryside as it rolled past our windows. There was a timeless tranquility about it, and the hectic hustle and bustle of life in the United States seemed a million miles away.

As professional psychologists, we still couldn't quite believe that we had flown thousands of miles to try to gain knowledge about our own profession from an old English gardener. I'm sure most of our friends would think we were crazy. How could we possibly explain that we had learned more about our profession by listening to the words of an old gardener who has had absolutely no training in our field than we had from our formal studies? Yet we think that what we had stumbled upon was astounding. Although at the time we had understood very little of what the gardener tried to explain to us, after we arrived home, the changes that began to occur in our lives were inconceivable. Literally, our lives made a stupendous shift for the better. Unbelievable as it sounds, my personal and family life changed overnight to something I had only dreamed was possible. The success in my work also increased dramatically. Janet's experience was similar; her already happy personal life became even better, and her success rate with clients also improved. The bizarre thing was that neither Janet nor I could explain why all these changes were taking place.

There was something exceptional about this gardener; his sense of security in what he said enhanced his credibility and increased the authority of his words. His air of confidence said, not arrogantly, but lovingly, "I'd love to help you." That's why Janet and I had returned to England. We hoped to engage him in further discussions on his philosophical and psychological beliefs, and to find out more about what seemed, to us, a mystery.

As Andy had predicted, the train ride was much more relaxing than traveling by car, and allowed us a far greater degree of freedom to appreciate the beauty of the English countryside we were passing through. The rolling hills dotted with sheep and the patchwork of fields basking in the sunshine seemed to welcome us back again. The slight rocking of the train had an almost hypnotic effect and we sat quietly, each immersed in our own thoughts, gazing out the carriage window.

After an hour or so, I mentioned to Janet, "My wife, Norma, will be joining me after our visit to Torquay. She's really looking forward to this vacation."

"When will she arrive?" Janet asked.

"The day we get back to London I pick her up at Heathrow Airport. I asked her if she wanted to come and spend some time with us in Torquay to meet Andy and Emily, but I think she felt a little shy and said she'd rather meet me later."

"I know you told me before," Janet said, smiling, "but remind me again. What are you two up to on this trip? Are you going to take England by storm?" Janet grinned. "You'd better be careful if you go bargain hunting down in Petticoat Lane. I don't know about you, but I still haven't got the dollar and pound values straight in my head," she said, laughing ruefully. "What appears to be a wonderful find here might not look like such a good deal when you get back to Denver and work out the exchange rate!"

"Well," I said, "forewarned is forearmed! I'll have to make sure we don't get carried away, but I don't think I stand a chance! Damage control is probably the best I can hope for," I said, chuckling. "We plan to stay five days in London and see all the famous places such as the Tower of London, Buckingham Palace, the British Museum and a host of other sights that Norma has been researching. Then, after our stay in London, we're heading north to a place called Newcastle where Norma has some distant relatives. Maybe we'll uncover some family secrets! Or on second thought, that might not be so good. Who knows what we could discover?"

"She must be quite excited at the thought of coming to England."

"Excited is hardly a strong enough word, Norma has been trying to figure out her wardrobe since the first day we decided to come and she's been reading everything she could lay her hands on about the areas we plan to visit."

Janet smiled warmly. "I know you'll both have a wonderful time."

After a three-and-a-half-hour journey through fields and the outskirts of towns, through cuts and around hills, by the backdoors of villages, catching quick glimpses of ancient cathedrals and minutes-long views of a rugged coastline and busy estuaries, the train finally pulled into Torquay, well named "The English Riviera." As planned, we quickly hailed a taxi to take us to the car rental office. Soon we were on our way to the Sea View Hotel where we would be spending the next few days.

We felt lucky to be back in England and were delighted by the unexpected sight of palm trees swaying in the ocean breeze. I had never imagined England with palm trees; I always thought it would be too cold. The very sight of them added to the holiday feeling of the town. Brightly striped awnings flapped over gaily painted shop fronts, inviting strolling tourists to view all kinds of wares. Everyone seemed to be having a good time, from the staid middle-aged couples walking hand in hand to the wandering young hippies in their Indian cotton clothes and dangling earrings. Their tousled appearance somehow added to the impression of childlike innocence, making it easier to understand their adamant belief that they could change the world—if only people would listen to their message.

The town's vibrancy was irresistible. In shop windows, bright pink sticks of rock candy vied with beautiful examples of Devonshire pottery, both enticing holidaymakers in to buy. We spent what remained of the day getting our bearings, wandering up one street and down the other on a slow voyage of discovery, until we could no longer function, then headed back to the hotel for a light supper and an early night.

Chapter Two
Renewing Our Acquaintance with Andy

*T*he following morning, I awoke to the sound of thunder and heavy rain pounding on the windows. What a contrast to the bright skies of the day before. I'd forgotten how changeable the English weather could be. After having a hearty English breakfast, I phoned Andy to let him know that we had arrived safe and sound.

It was lovely to hear his soft English voice again welcoming Janet and me back to England. He expressed the wish that our holiday would be both joyful and fruitful, then recommended that we should have a good rest after our long trip. "Perhaps we could get together tomorrow for lunch at the Crown Inn?" Janet and I agreed that was a sensible idea, so Andy gave us directions and we arranged to meet him there at noon the following day. A restful day sounded good to both of us, since we were still suffering a little from jet lag.

Outside, the streets were running like rivers but luckily by ten o'clock the rain had vanished and the sun came out. Janet suggested that a walk would feel good after sitting so much during the last couple of days so we set out on a walk to a nearby village to stretch our legs and do a little sightseeing. We visited countless shops, buying the usual post cards and trinkets to take home. After wandering aimlessly for a few hours, I felt absolutely exhausted, although Janet, being younger and slimmer, was ready to enjoy a few more hours of sightseeing. Regretfully admitting to myself that I was no longer a youngster and that she had me beat, I returned to crawl off to bed by six-thirty.

After a sound sleep I woke to sun streaming in the window at eight the following morning, refreshed and ready to go. I enjoyed a leisurely breakfast and strolled the grounds for a while, then looked over some brochures describing local highlights while I waited for Janet to join me. The couple running our hotel assured us that the Crown Inn was only a little way down the road, and within easy walking distance. At least, that's what they said. We found out that day, however, that our idea of "just down the road" and the English view was vastly different. When we finally arrived at the Crown Inn, we were bushed and parched by the mid-day sun. Even Janet was a little the worse for wear and grateful that we had arrived at our destination. By this time the sun and wind had dried all signs of yesterday's downpour, so we decided to take an outside table beneath a magnificent oak tree. The waitress suggested we should try the lager beer to quench our thirsts and so, while we waited for Andy, I tried the beer and Janet ordered lemonade. After our strenuous hike, it felt good to relax with a cold drink in the shade of the huge old oak.

"Everything seems so old and yet so timeless here, doesn't it?" Janet remarked as she touched a hand to the bark. "It's like it's been here forever. I wonder what stories this old tree could tell if it could speak."

As we settled into the peaceful atmosphere of the garden, lulled by the hum of bees busy at work in the flowers, we discussed some of Andy's unusual philosophical beliefs and agreed that it was wonderful that our associates were starting to see the value of what we had learned from the gardener.

Janet and I had come on a particular mission: to find out more about the *Three Principles* that Andy calls *Mind, Consciousness* and *Thought*. His claim that these *Three Principles* hold the secret to all psychological functioning intrigued Janet and me. Fascinated by his theories and ideas, we discussed the many changes in our lives and practices since we first met this remarkable gardener. Since then both of us had seen people experience remarkable cures; people we thought would be in therapy for years underwent positive, beneficial change, literally before our eyes.

We talked about the strange, insecure feeling engendered by seeing clients change so quickly as they started to understand the correlation between their own thoughts and their behavior. We laughed when we both admitted how unnerved we had been to realize that we didn't really understand how the changes came about.

"Then it came to me," Janet mused. "It had to be what we were saying to them about their thoughts."

"I had the same sort of incidents as you, Janet, and for the life of me I couldn't figure out what was happening to some of my clients. What we are saying about people's thoughts and consciousness seems so simple, yet the results are so positive."

Moments later, we heard a familiar voice. "Welcome to England!"

It was Andy, seemingly as timeless as the old oak tree under which we sat. He looked just the same as when we had seen him before, his kind face beaming as his gnarled hand grasped mine in greeting.

"Well, this is a pleasure, I must say," he said, chuckling as Janet gave him a big hug and kissed his cheek.

"You have no idea how delighted I am to be in England again, and especially to be seeing you," she said warmly.

Andy smiled shyly at Janet's words and said he felt the same pleasure at seeing both of us. When we were all seated again, the waitress bustled over and asked Andy what he would like to drink.

"That lemonade looks like it would fill the bill. I'd love one."

Janet remarked that she had forgotten how beautiful England was. There was a moment's quiet while we all enjoyed the beauty of the summer garden. The waitress returned with Andy's drink and took our lunch order, then our conversation resumed.

I asked after Andy's wife, Emily.

"Emily is doing very well and looking forward to seeing both of you again. She's hoping that you can find the time to come and visit us for lunch."

We thanked him for the invitation and assured him that we would be honored.

"And the more time we can spend with you the better!" Janet said enthusiastically.

Andy smiled at her words, then pretended to take a big, long-suffering sigh. "Now, Janet, you've traveled halfway round the world to ask some questions, so you'd better start asking."

"Well, Andy," Janet said as she tossed her long auburn hair away from her face, "I can't express the feelings of gratefulness I have for the time we shared together last time I was in England. I've thought so often about some of the fascinating things you said.

But I must admit, at times I have experienced difficulty following the deeper meaning of your philosophy."

"In what way?" Andy asked.

"It's really difficult for me to explain. Okay! Let's put it this way. As you know, Andy, I'm a marriage counselor and I can't believe the incredible results I've been getting in my office."

Andy grinned and asked Janet if she was bragging or complaining.

Janet's face glowed as she said, "No, no, no. It's nothing like that. Let me try to explain it this way. I remember the last time I was in England, you suggested to me that as far as you are concerned, trying to help people by taking them back into their past was looking in the wrong direction for the answer.

"At first your words baffled me, because as you know, we were taught to take people back into their past to find out where their troubles originated. Now it's becoming more and more apparent to me that you were correct when you said that I was going in the wrong direction to find what I was trying to achieve.

"This story might interest you. One day I was working with a client who had considerable problems in his marriage. I could see that the man was suffering and I really wanted to help him. Then I noticed, the more I talked to him about his negative past, the more depressed he became and the more

I commiserated with him in his bad feelings, the worse he became. Right there and then, I remembered what you had said about going back into the past being psychological suicide. At that moment I realized that as I commiserated with my clients, not only was I not helping them, I was becoming a mental wreck myself.

"That was a turning point for me, and from that moment on, I changed my ways. Now I take my clients to more positive feelings and you wouldn't believe the difference it makes."

The old gardener smiled but made no comment. It was obvious that Janet was enjoying telling Andy all about her success as she continued. "About the same time, I had another client who had been in therapy for over a year, and that's when I really realized that taking him back into the past was only upsetting him. I thought about you and started to explain to him as well as I could about the *Three Principles*. To my absolute astonishment he started to cry, then thanked me for what I had said to him. I sat there wondering what in the world the man was talking about and asked him exactly what I had said to create such a reaction.

"Then he started to explain to *me* what the principles really meant to him and how he had just realized that it was only his own thoughts that were creating his problem. He obviously understood the meaning behind the *Three Principles* better than I did.

"Finally out of sheer embarrassment I stopped his explanation and asked him, laughingly, 'Who's the doctor here, you or me?'

"Now this man is mentally healthier and more stable than most people I know."

Andy smiled hugely but again refrained from making any comment.

Janet continued, "What baffles me is that I know it works and I've helped some people beyond my wildest dreams, but still it mystifies me." She wrinkled her brow in bewilderment. "It's like one big psychological puzzle."

Andy laughed at her confused look and replied, "You are the therapists, not me. Never in a million years would I ever tell anyone such as you what to do, or what not to do. I am simply telling you about the existence of the principles and how they work, and you are talking about what you do with them. One is before the creation of any form; the other is strictly form. But, just maybe if we listen to each other with open minds, we can come up with something that will help both of us to understand how the form and the formless are attached to each other. Who knows? You may find the answer to your own question."

I admitted that I was in the same boat as Janet and didn't understand how all this worked. "I do understand to a certain degree, how my thoughts have a lot to do with how I relate to life, but, like Janet, I have a problem getting the big picture. I want to hear more about how, precisely, this would help a marriage."

Andy smiled and looked up at the passing clouds. "My advice to anyone who is looking for help in their marriage would be to seek help from someone who sees life in a positive way or gives out positive advice."

"But where do you find such people?" I asked.

"Believe me, Eric, such people are everywhere; it could be your neighbor, a friend, your doctor, your minister or your therapist. Look for a stable, contented person who lives in a higher state of well-being.

"I suggest looking for a person who sees life with a positive attitude, not someone who is full of negativity. A person with a negative outlook would just be the typical case of the blind leading the blind. When you find this positive individual, listen very carefully to his advice, because his experience and common sense will no doubt be very useful to you."

At this point, the waitress came with our food, and we continued talking while we ate.

"Andy," Janet asked, "would you explain again what you mean when you say that delving into the past is so detrimental in therapy? Maybe if you could say it in a different way I'll be able to get it on a deeper level."

"First of all, Janet, I'd like you to understand, I'm not talking to you as a therapist. Again I'm talking in the *impersonal*, and the *impersonal* pertains to everyone on this earth, not just the chosen few."

Janet and I were dumbfounded by the certainty in Andy's voice, and neither of us knew what to say. Then Andy said, "Think about it for a moment, then tell me how much of our past exists as reality now, other than our memories? And what are memories?"

Again neither Janet nor I could offer a reply, so Andy continued. "Memories are only old, ghostly thoughts carried through time and actually have nothing to do with the *now*."

I asked Andy if he remembered our friend Tom who had been with us last year.

"Which one was Tom?" he asked.

"Remember? He was the one who vigorously disagreed with you regarding such statements and is a staunch believer in the Freudian concept of going into the past to fix problems."

"Was he the tall, young intellect who couldn't listen for constantly asking questions? Or was he the gentleman who appeared to be rather unhappy all the time?"

"That's him," Janet replied, "the one who always seemed to be unhappy."

"Yes I remember him. How is he doing?"

"Eric and I were talking about him just the other day," Janet replied. "He's doing remarkably well these days. Since his visit to the conference in England last year, he has semi-retired and does a lot of fishing with his son, and he's even undergoing treatment for his drinking problem. As a matter of fact, he's currently writing a book called 'Investigating the Past to Fix the Present'."

Andy closed his eyes and smiled in amusement on hearing the name of Tom's new book.

"Next time you see him, please give him my regards."

"I will," replied Janet. "You know Andy, it's the strangest thing. He talks highly of you and thinks you're a great guy, and in fact, believes that some of the things you said helped him. Yet, at the same time, he completely disagrees with almost everything he heard you say. Especially when you said, 'Going back into your negative past to find happiness is psychological suicide.' That really got him upset."

Andy listened intently to Janet, then when she was finished, he replied, "May I suggest to you that it would be to your best advantage to forget all about what Tom thinks, or what anyone else thinks? Believe me, Janet, it is far more beneficial to care what *you* think.

"What Tom perceives of life is his reality, just as you perceive your reality. What many fail to understand is that all past experiences are now only ghostly thoughts carried through time. Seeing this frees you from the phantom illusions and memories that hold you a prisoner of your now deceased past.

> *"Waste not your time in the paths*
> *Of yesterday's negative memories,*
> *For they are but illusions in time,*
> *Controlling how you perceive life now."*

After a lengthy pause Andy continued, "You should observe people as whole and healthy, not as a product of their past. Otherwise you would be just as much a prisoner of the past as your client; I believe you just called that commiserating.

"What you have to realize, Janet, is that

> *"Negative memories dampen*
> *the human spirit and*
> *Prevent one from seeing*
> *the beauty of today."*

Chapter Three
The Importance of the Now

*A*s soon as Andy was out of sight Janet asked, "Do you understand why Andy places such importance on not going into the past and the importance of the *now*?"

"I don't know, Janet, but I have a strange feeling that there's more to this than meets the eye. We've explained to Andy time and time again that we no longer take clients back into their negative life and how successful that has been for us. Yet he still talks to us about the importance of the *now*."

"Why do you suppose that is?" Janet asked. "Do you think he doesn't see that we're already aware of this?"

"I have a funny feeling that Andy is fully aware of what we know about our thoughts," I replied, "and right now I have the feeling that he is about to give us a talk on what we don't know."

Andy returned to the table carrying another round of lemonades and re-seated himself. No sooner was he back than Janet asked, "Andy, why do you put so much importance in not getting caught up in the past?"

He looked straight into Janet's eyes and asked. "Why do you think many of the wise throughout time have tried to explain to us the importance of living in the *now*?"

"I don't know," she muttered in frustration.

"Truthfully, I've often wondered that myself," I answered. "As a matter of fact, when I travelled through India and Nepal, many of the teachers talked about the importance of living in the *now*, but I could never understand its importance. Andy, why do *you* think the wise put so much value on the *now*?"

Andy took a sip of his lemonade before he replied, "Because, *now* is really all there is or ever will be. Now is every moment of every day in perfect motion."

His words surprised me. I felt that I had to question his certainty. I asked him, "How can you say, *now* is every moment of every day in perfect motion, when all over the world there are such horrible things happening? What about the war in Vietnam, for example, where such needless suffering is going on right now? And what about the assassinations of innocent people, presidents and leaders, people who try to give the world some hope?"

There seemed to be so much disenchantment in the world that I really hoped that Andy would come up with an answer that I could understand and accept.

Andy scratched his head thoughtfully. After a pause, to my surprise he replied,

> *"Now is not a thing that is tangible.*
> *Now is neither yesterday nor tomorrow.*
> *Now is a fleeting moment in time and is*
> *completely neutral.*
> *Now is all there really is or ever will be.*

"What you have to realize is, living in the *now* is living without negative thoughts from past traumas contaminating your thought system, thoughts that prevent you from seeing what-is, instead of what-isn't.

> *"It is the now that takes you from living in the darkness*
> *of yesterday's negative memories*
> *And turns the darkness into light.*
> *Remember, my friend,*
> *Darkness cannot survive in the midst of light*
> *And living in the now is that light."*

The gardener's words were so far beyond my immediate comprehension that I felt I would definitely need time to think about what he had just said. But despite that, I had to admit there was an undeniably beautiful feeling present; it was the same feeling that I had experienced the last time I was with Andy. I didn't know what I was learning, but I was sure that I was picking up something, and it felt wonderful.

Janet, eyes shining, blurted out that she just had to ask one more question. "What did you mean when you said, 'preventing us from seeing what-is, instead of what-isn't'?"

Andy chuckled at her excitement. "The way I see it, Luv, if your head is filled with negative memories and unhappy historical events, they override what is really happening today and never allow you to see today with any clarity. I can guarantee you that while you look through so much ghostly contamination, you will never, never, know the beauty of living in the *now.*"

Janet rubbed her chin as though that would help her to understand. Noticing her bewilderment, Andy said, "I can see that the penny hasn't dropped yet."

"You're right, Andy, I'm afraid I still don't get what you mean."

In a soft voice Andy suggested, "Maybe we could try another tack. Let me try to explain it this way. People's past negative experiences are not the problem; the problem lies in constantly *thinking* about them.

"If you remember, this is what I tried to tell you the last time you were here in England, that we live in a world governed by our own thoughts. Our thoughts create the reality that we, personally, experience. This is why I say the secret to all happiness and all social problems lies deep within the recesses of our *own* inner knowledge, waiting to be uncovered. And this is why it is very important not to be afraid to change your mind and see a more positive life. I am sure in your life you have met stubborn people who claim with great pride that once they make up their mind about something, they never give in and change it; or others who won't change their minds or apologize for some wrong they have done, because they believe that an apology is a sign of weakness."

I laughed out loud. "Almost every day of my life," I acknowledged ruefully.

Janet said that she, too, regularly ran into this problem with stubborn people who couldn't, or wouldn't, apologize even if their life depended on it. "As far as I'm concerned," she smiled, "having the graciousness to say you are sorry is usually a sign of courage, not to mention a big relief."

"That is very wise of you, Janet," Andy said, patting her arm, "and I agree with you one hundred percent. One has to bend with the wind and be sufficiently flexible to change, otherwise you will always be a prisoner of your own innocently negative way of thinking.

"Again, I say to you, the secret to such change lies in the proper use of *Mind, Consciousness* and *Thought*. When used properly, they are the mystical trio that will lead you to the knowledge you seek."

As Andy said these words, an unbelievable feeling welled up within me and when I looked over at Janet, I was not really surprised to see her face full of emotion, her eyes brimming with tears. The notion that there really was hope for all my clients who were looking for help overwhelmed me. I knew that Janet felt the same. She voiced just what I was thinking. "Wouldn't it give so many people hope if they could only understand that simple statement. I still don't understand; it's more of a feeling."

"I know what you mean Janet, I'm in the same boat as you."

Andy pushed his plate aside, got up and walked to the edge of the courtyard, apparently totally preoccupied with the climbing roses that were spilling toward us over the low stone wall. "Aren't these wonderful?" he commented. "Whoever is looking after this garden really cares and it shows. It does my heart good to see plants loved and cared for this way."

Andy returned to the table, lowered his long frame into his chair, then asked, "How is your other friend, Peter, getting on these days?"

"I'm sorry to tell you that Peter had a nervous breakdown about two months ago and gave up on his profession. He's now following some guru in the Nevada desert, on a search for Spiritual Truth."

I told him that over the past several months Peter's expertise had been called on regularly in various trials, until he had gradually become a professional witness.

"What, exactly, is a professional witness? I didn't know there was such a thing."

"Well, he works in the courts for either the prosecution or the defense, giving his professional opinion," I explained. "He would go to court and testify on behalf of various clients, but the constant need to contradict himself to suit each different client eventually caused him so much distress that he felt he could no longer, in conscience, carry on."

"I'm truly sorry to hear that, Eric. He is such a nice young man." Andy shook his head. "The poor soul must have gone through a lot of torment to give up his profession."

"The sad part is, his intentions were always good. And look at him now, he's a basket case," Janet added.

"That is too bad," Andy said as he stood up. "Well, if you'll excuse me, I'll have to leave you folks for now and take care of some errands. So we'll see you tomorrow. Thank you for a wonderful lunch."

Janet gave him a hug and I thanked him for his time and mentioned that we were looking forward to seeing Emily again.

Once Andy was out of earshot, Janet burst out laughing and said, "Welcome back to England! Wasn't that amazing?"

I joined in her laughter, shaking my head in wonderment. "Do you know, Janet, I'd forgotten what it was like to talk with Andy."

"I know what you mean, Eric. What gets me is his confidence and the nonchalant way he talks, as if he could care less whether we understood what he said or not. Tell me, did you understand everything Andy said when he talked about the importance of living in the *now*?"

"Not fully, but I could see that somehow it has to do with disconnecting ourselves from our past negative memories and not continuing to beat ourselves up over them."

"You know, Eric, I'm just starting to get a glimmer of a deeper understanding of what is happening in our office and why some of my clients have been changing. You know what it is? It's because they are dropping a lot of their psychological baggage from the past."

Janet was absolutely right, and just sitting there thinking about it filled me with the most beautiful feelings of gratitude and amazement.

Janet got up to leave to take in some more sights. "I'll see you at the hotel about six for dinner," she said, and left me to ponder Andy's words and bask in the warmth of my pleasant feelings.

Chapter Four
The Three Principles

*J*anet and I decided to take a morning to explore some more of Torquay. It was wonderful to smell the ocean breeze as wheeling seagulls called, searching for the day's meal, while we mingled with other tourists out enjoying the summer morning. There was a feeling of gaiety and light-heartedness everywhere and across the bay Babbecombe Beach stretched out in an inviting crescent of gold, enticing holiday makers to open up deck chairs and spread blankets on the sand. We sat for a while, soaking up the heat of the sun in blissful peace and quiet. My thoughts turned to Andy and his words of wisdom. I felt so grateful for all that had happened since the first time we'd talked with him. I definitely had no reservations about taking this trip to meet him again; I suspected that it was one of the most worthwhile things I could ever do.

After a few more minutes, we sauntered on and came to the Princess Gardens, a bright profusion of flowers interspersed with green lawns and neatly trimmed pathways.

Janet had taken to photography with her usual enthusiasm for life, managing to capture some exquisite scenes with her camera. Now, she insisted on my posing in front of a stunning rhododendron bush laden with blush pink flowers. As I was trying to decide on my most photogenic angle, I heard a chuckle behind me.

"I hope you have insurance on that camera!"

I turned around and there was Andy, cheerily smiling at us.

"Well, for heaven's sake," Janet laughed. "What are you doing here? I bet you heard about the famous American photographer visiting the area and you wanted to be in one of her pictures."

"Not exactly," Andy said, grinning. "You just happened to have discovered one of my favorite spots. I try to get over here once or twice a week to see how the plants are doing."

Janet was not going to take "no" for an answer and before we knew it, the old gardener and I were being added to her collection of shots.

"Jack would never forgive me if I didn't bring home some snaps. He so wanted to come but was too busy with the second store. It already seems years since we were together," she said wistfully.

"Anyway," she brightened, "this is a great way to share a little bit of what's been happening."

We meandered along the path for a while and then I suggested we might go for a coffee if Andy could take the time. He recommended the distinguished old Torbay Hotel as the spot to get an excellent coffee. After the brightness of the day, I was ready for a sit down in the cool dining room.

"Andy, I don't know if you already know this, but in the 1800s there was a well-known psychologist by the name of William James who was widely regarded as the father of psychology. In 1890 he published a work called *The Principles of Psychology* that referred to psychology as a science. He indicated that his work was exploratory and he knew he didn't have the answer he was searching for. He hoped and dreamed that some day someone would discover the principles that would change psychology from a philosophy into a working science, principles that would assist the field to better understand and control the cause and effect of mental health. He felt if ever such a discovery were made it would change psychology on a monumental scale. Janet and I have been talking this over and we think maybe you have discovered these principles. Isn't that right, Janet?"

Nodding her head enthusiastically, Janet exclaimed, "Yes, I think so." Then she began shaking her head, "Wow, isn't this unbelievable?"

"That's very interesting, Eric, and I feel very honored that you would make such a statement, but I'm afraid I know nothing about this William James you speak of, or his psychological theories. But I can tell you this: The *Three Principles* of *Universal Mind*, *Universal Consciousness* and *Universal Thought* are most definitely the principles that turn psychology from a guesswork philosophy into a working science."

"Wouldn't it have been wonderful, Andy, if William James could have known that his dream of finding the elusive principles had come true and had actually become a reality?"

Suddenly Janet sat bolt upright and exclaimed, "Do you know what, Eric? I just realized that I used to think that each mental illness was different and required unique treatment!

"Now I am starting to see that they are essentially one generic condition with many different disguises and the very essence of all mental illnesses is a *deluded thought* that is relied on as reality.

"You know, Eric, we all characterize each different type of thought and each different behavior that originates from the different thoughts as separate types of illnesses—as separate areas of specialization.

"For example, if you applied the field of psychology's logic to a worrier, every particular problem that he worried about, whether it be his finances, his job, or whether or not his car will start today, would be seen as a separate area of specialization. Rather, all his problems should be seen as outgrowths of his own thoughts, and not as reality."

I was impressed with Janet's understanding. "You know, Janet, I never quite saw it that way before, but you're correct. Take a phobic person who is deathly afraid of heights, that most definitely would be his thoughts in action."

Janet joined in again, "What about a grossly underweight anorexic who is deathly afraid that consuming a one ounce piece of meat will make her fat? Or a person with an obsessive compulsive disorder who must return to the house fifteen times every morning to make sure that the front door is locked? Now I'm starting to see that when these thoughts are given the full weight of reality and acted upon, they are the cause of the pathological behavior.

"On the other hand if these thoughts didn't appear in their minds these people would not be symptomatic. Or, if the thoughts appeared and were seen as just thoughts, not as realities, the clients would not be categorized as having various mental illnesses. If they took these thoughts in stride rather than reacting to them so strongly we wouldn't say they were mentally ill. There need only be one generic mental illness: an inability to see the role of *Thought*."

Janet was excited by her new-found, deeper understanding. "I think I know now, Eric, how we and the other members of our staff are bringing our clients a better understanding of their own role in creating the reality they live in. Wow! Now I know why I came back to England."

The gardener, who had been the picture of serenity, broke into a pleased smile as he congratulated both of us for having such wisdom.

I thought to myself, "What has happened in my life that changed my way of looking at reality? Sometimes in the past couple of years I would shake my head in disbelief at the results that we were getting at the clinic."

I shared the thought with Janet and Andy, then remarked, "But others in the field can't seem to believe our successes either. I often wonder if the field as a whole will ever look at the *Three Principles*." Andy smiled at my words. "You have no idea the joy it brings me to see both of you so happy and hearing the wonderful results you are getting with your work.

"I feel sure you know by now that I am not belittling anyone's teachings when I'm talking about the principles and the need to forget delving into the past. As a matter of fact, I am not talking about anybody in particular, nor am I talking about any group. I am talking in the *impersonal* and with all my heart and soul I admire people such as you two and your entire profession, who put your own mental well-being in jeopardy each and every day talking to people who are lost in a maze of mental instability."

Our conversation paused, then resumed with Janet thanking Andy for his kind words. Then she said, "You know Andy, one of the questions we get asked most often is why you limit the principles to only three. Why couldn't there be more?"

Andy answered, "Because, Luv, the *Three Principles* are the trinity of all psychological experience and with these *Three Principles* we weave our entire experience here on earth."

"But why can't there be more than three principles?" Janet repeated.

"I just told you. They are the principles that create *all* human experience here on earth."

Andy waited for Janet to say something more, but she made no response. He then asked us to try to figure out anything that could possibly be conceived in this reality without using the *Three Principles* just mentioned; or indeed, to think of anything else that could be considered a principle.

"What about our emotions," I asked "or our feelings or our insecurities?"

Andy studied us as he rubbed his chin for a moment, then asked us to reconsider that question. "How could you have an emotion without knowing

40

about it? How could you be aware of this conversation without using your mind, your consciousness and your thoughts? Your emotions, your feelings and your insecurities are all products of the *Three Principles*, therefore they cannot be considered as principles themselves."

Then, with a patient smile, he said, "I'll tell you again. The principles allow us to experience life in totality. The very moment you try to think of another principle, that is my checkmate."

"Why do you say that?" I asked, still struggling to figure out his meaning.

"Eric, the simple fact that you are able to ask such a question proves you are using the *Three Principles* to ask the question. Think about it for a minute and you will see that you have to have the power of *Mind* and you have to be *Conscious* and you have to have *Thought* to relate to life.

"Anything else is a product of their usage. Therefore, it is virtually impossible to think of any mental activity that isn't a product of the principles."

I was getting ready to challenge him on that statement when I hesitated for a moment. Then it became clear to me that Andy was correct; we do have to have a mind, we do have to be conscious and we do have to think in order to be aware of our lives, our realities. I asked him if he would be kind enough to explain what he was trying to tell me in another way.

"Eric, if you want my advice I would say this: Look carefully. Investigate how you, as a free-thinking agent, use the three universal gifts of *Mind*, *Consciousness* and *Thought* to perceive the reality you live in every second of every day. Here is the formula that will give you a solid foundation on which to build your search and assist you to find many of the answers you seek:

"*Mind* + *Consciousness* + *Thought* = Reality.

"These *Three Principles* lead to the secret of all psychological functioning."

Listening to the gardener talk was fascinating, and I felt I was grasping the *Three Principles*, but somehow I still failed to understand the magnitude of the importance he was placing on them. "Andy, I just don't see how a psychological science can be created out of just three principles!"

Andy laughed and said, "There's really only One." Then he just smiled benevolently at me, awaiting my reaction.

As his eyes met mine, it suddenly came to me. I related, "When I was in school one of my professors once explained to the class that there are four principles in arithmetic: addition, subtraction, multiplication and division. Then he went on to explain to us, that in arithmetic we consider the principles as separate entities. Yet if you look very closely you will see that there is only one principle—addition—used in different ways."

Janet immediately threw up her arms, exclaiming, "Hold it, Eric! What in heaven's name do you mean, all four of the principles in arithmetic are just one?"

"The way it was told to me was that it is easier for most people to think of the processes as being totally different than to think of them as addition turned around."

"Talk about being turned around. That's where this talk has me. Eric, all the time I've known you, I never thought you knew so many little facts. I'm truly impressed."

Andy said, "I find the statement that arithmetic has only one principle fascinating, and really that is what I'm saying about *Mind, Consciousness* and *Thought*. They are the trinity of all human experience, they are one principle in three forms. But the fact remains that the principles of mathematics wouldn't exist at all if it weren't for the *Three Principles* of *Mind, Consciousness* and *Thought*."

"Whew," Janet breathed.

Andy just smiled knowingly, and once again I felt like I'd just been caught with my hand in the cookie jar. "Andy, am I hearing you correctly? Are you saying that there is really only one principle and the other two are just there to explain its workings?" I asked.

"Exactly," Andy replied.

"Then in you estimation, which one is most important?"

"If all three are the same, then all three must be equally important."

Janet, who had been sitting quietly, looking from me to Andy and back to me again during the last conversation, spoke up. "Your answer was totally heavy, Andy. It's going to require a good bit of time and a good bit of thinking to even begin to absorb what you're saying."

Andy replied, "You know, Luv, the next time you think of investigating the *Three Principles* you might find it very interesting if you consider looking into their true nature—not how they work, but the simple fact that they exist.

"Try to see that every human being on this planet functions using the same three gifts. Now remember, on their own, these gifts are completely neutral. It is how we, as human beings, personally use them that is significant in our lives.

"And, remember, both of you: The *Three Principles* I speak of are universal constants that can never change and are never separate entities from us. From the cradle to the grave, they totally encompass the reality we observe and experience in this lifetime."

Janet admitted that she was still somewhat baffled by the concept of the *Three Principles*, and felt that there was definitely more to them than she currently understood. Andy smiled kindly at her. "Delving into the *Three Principles* is endless. Don't ever believe, as many do, that just because you can remember the three words, *Mind*, *Consciousness* and *Thought*, you will gain the understanding you seek. My pet parrot could repeat the words, but just knowing them by rote wouldn't do him any good— any more than your knowing them intellectually does you any good.

"Even more disastrous would be to try to connect this understanding with some of your techniques, ideas and concepts. If you do this, I can guarantee you will surely fail."

Andy smiled as he caught Janet trying to hide a yawn, "What do you say we take a rest and indulge in another cup of tea?"

Chapter Five
Universal Consciousness

*A*fter fifteen minutes of laughter and small talk and a steaming cup of strong English tea, I asked, "Andy, why do you think our friend Tom listened to the same words we did last year, and yet he didn't seem to understand anything about his own thoughts creating many of his problems? Can you explain that?"

Andy paused thoughtfully for a moment before he answered. "You have to remember, Eric, that just like you, Tom is committed to his own views on life. Like many others Tom feels he was trained in a different understanding altogether and, as you already know, Tom isn't ready to listen to anything new."

"But we all seem to find it so difficult to understand what our ears are hearing, Andy. Why do you think this is so?"

Pointing to the sky Andy replied, "The knowledge you seek regarding human behavior is beyond the written or spoken word. This is why I ask you to look for a deeper dimension of *Thought*.

"The trouble is, not too many understand the enormous difference between one's personal thoughts and the universal principle called *Thought.*

"However, this I can guarantee you, no matter who you are in this life, such knowledge can only be uncovered from deep within your own inner consciousness."

Once again Janet had been quietly listening to me and Andy, but now she broke in with a question. "Andy, could you clarify what you mean by *Universal Consciousness?*"

Andy shook his head. "Janet, no one, but no one, can ever explain intellectually what *Universal Consciousness* really is.

"Yet, as thinking human beings, we use this magnificent gift every day of our lives. It's a gift that enables us to experience the existence of creation.

"I guess you could say: it just is."

"Andy, I'm sorry if I seem to keep asking the same question again and again," Janet apologized, "but it's really important to me to better understand the principles. Why do you differentiate between *Universal Consciousness* and personal consciousness?"

The gardener thought for a considerable time, then answered. "My dear, *Universal Consciousness* has no form of its own and can only be talked about metaphorically. Let me try to explain it this way. *Universal Consciousness* is a gift we use to travel through this life.

It allows us to see creation. It's a psychological gift that comes from before time, space or matter. As far as you are concerned, this world would not exist without it.

"Personal consciousness is a gift that we use from moment to moment to see and react to the world we live in."

I found Andy's answer very interesting, but what really held my attention was the assurance with which he spoke, the confidence in his voice, as though what he had just said was a straightforward and simple fact.

Looking very serious, Janet remarked, "So what I hear you saying, Andy, is that this knowledge or understanding we are looking for is found in a zone beyond time, space and matter?"

"Yes, that's what I'm saying."

"Hmm. Well, I have to say, what you are saying is amazing to me but I'm afraid I don't get this talk about time, space and matter. Do you think you could elaborate a little more on the idea of something beyond time, space and matter?" Janet asked.

There was a moment of quiet while Andy looked down at his hands. "I'm afraid not. How could anyone elaborate on something that is before form?

"What you have to realize, Janet, is that the wisdom of the sages was beyond explanation with mere words and had to be spoken of metaphorically.

This is where many get mixed up in their thinking, they often take the metaphor as literal truth and, most definitely, this will only lead away from what is sought.

"Perhaps that's true," I said, joining in, "but the big question is, how do we access this knowledge?"

Andy gazed at me intently and said, "Eric,

> *"When your mind is still enough*
> *And goes into the state of no personal thought,*
> *The incubation takes place*
> *And the wisdom you seek will be brought to life."*

Reluctantly I admitted, "Andy, I can't deny that your words intrigue me, but much of the time I have little or no idea what in heaven's name you're talking about. And, I've been wondering what spiritual truths have to do with psychology."

"What I have been saying to you Eric, has *everything* to do with psychology. Right now we are discussing the essence of every human being's psychological make-up."

I told him that I could not connect what he was talking about to our profession.

Andy looked at me and sighed heavily. "Eric, what many don't realize is that,

> *"When our thoughts are working strictly*
> *from the human plane,*
> *We are somewhere between the physical plane*
> *and the spiritual plane,*
> *And this is where the confusion and lostness*
> *of humanity prevails.*

"Another way to say the same thing would be that when we are using our personal minds from the lower levels of consciousness, we are using the power of the egotistical self, which inevitably leads to mental suffering and the same old problems that have plagued humanity since the beginning of time.

"On the other hand, when we are using the gift of the *Universal Mind* properly, we are using the power of our own innate wisdom and this is where the secret to all knowledge lies.

"By delving into sickness too much, and ignoring the mental health that lies within, you will build a belief system on a quagmire riddled with quicksand.

"What you and Janet fail to see is that you are concentrating on trying to find out how people think or what they think, when you should be looking at the fact *that* people think.

"One is after the form and the other is before the form. Therefore the understanding of the *Three Principles* is both a cure and a prevention for the errors that may occur in the human thought system. These same *Three Principles* connect psychology and psychiatry as having the same quest, 'To help the client.' They are the missing link that changes psychology from a philosophy into a working science."

"Well, Andy, I'm impressed by your confidence. But how can you be so sure of what you are saying?"

Andy smiled. "I can no more tell you the answer to that question than fly to the moon, but I can assure you that if you could see the simplicity beyond my words you would understand the answer on your own."

I made no response as his words had once again left me speechless, yet never had I felt so invigorated and filled to the brim with wonderful feelings.

There was a long reflective silence, broken when Janet asked Andy if he would give us his definition of *Mind*.

Without any hesitation he replied, "My definition of *Mind*?

> *"Mind is the spiritual power that*
> *activates the human brain.*
> *Mind is one of the greatest mysteries on earth."*

"Can you explain such a phenomenon?" Janet asked.

"Janet, I just told you. *Mind* is one of the greatest mysteries on earth and cannot be explained by mere words."

Andy's words reminded me of a professor I had had in college who once said to me, "Many people who have reached higher dimensions of understanding have answers that are simple and quotable, and yet they rarely satisfy the intellect that is trying to figure it all out."

As if he could read my mind, Andy advised me to stop trying to figure it all out and, instead, to let my mind be silent and just—be. Then, with a huge grin on his face, he said, "Simplicity takes little effort, yet it's remarkable how simplicity often appears to be clever and unfathomable. Interesting to think about, isn't it?"

Janet glanced over at me, raised her eyebrows and breathed, "Wow!" and commented that Andy uttered more metaphors and conundrums than any one else she she'd ever known.

I felt that Andy must be getting fed up with us for repeatedly asking the same questions, but I had to ask him if he would be kind enough to explain his theory regarding the *Three Principles* just one more time.

Andy smiled, "I'd be happy to, Eric. Here's the way I see it. A principle is an original spiritual source before form.

"There are three principles: *Mind, Consciousness and Thought.* By using these three gifts, we create in our heads what we think of life as a whole. All our beliefs, ideas, concepts, doctrines, in fact literally everything on earth is a direct result of our usage of the *Three Principles.*

"And, it's very important that you remember:

"Any doctrine that is created from the principles is not the principles, but a form the principles have taken on."

"Andy, correct me if I'm wrong. You're saying all ideas, concepts and techniques are created from the principles. The techniques, however, are in themselves not the principles. Is that right?"

"Absolutely correct," Andy replied.

"Hmm. In that case, how much value do you place on techniques?"

"Techniques will not help you to find the knowledge or the happiness you seek. I would call techniques *the lost man's way to enlightenment.*

"This, my friends, I can assure you. If you ever meet teachers who are using techniques to explain the workings of the principles, they have absolutely no idea what they are talking about and will undoubtedly lead you astray."

"Why do you say that?" I asked.

Andy heaved another deep sigh, then explained. "The *Three Principles* are not of this world and yet, paradoxically, nothing would exist for us in this world if we didn't have them.

"They permeate both the existence of the form and the formless. However, if you ever try to explain the *Three Principles* via a technique, then the essence of the principles will be taking on a form."

I certainly didn't fully understand Andy's explanation about the *Three Principles* not being of this world. Nevertheless, I wasn't about to keep bugging by asking him more questions. I was full to the brim with such a calm feeling that instinctively I knew that I'd had sufficient for one day.

Andy noticed my condition, smiled sympathetically and patted me on the shoulder. "I think we should call it a day," he said. "What do you say we meet tomorrow. Is there anywhere special you'd like to go?"

"There's a place I've been dying to visit!" Janet exclaimed. "Would it be alright with you if we get together at Powderham Castle?"

"Excellent choice," Andy agreed.

"We'll pick you up and we can all drive over together," I said, "if that suits you."

"Certainly, that sounds like a sensible plan. We'll see you about ten," said Andy as he took his leave.

Chapter Six
Universal Mind

When we arrived at their cottage Andy and Emily appeared at the door looking like two kids anticipating a picnic.

It took about an hour to reach our destination. We turned off the main road into a long driveway overhung by huge old trees, crossed an arched stone bridge and entered the outer courtyard where we parked with two or three other cars.

Although called a castle, Powderham falls more into the classification of fortified house. Nonetheless, nothing could have prepared us for the feeling of history embodied in the splendid old building surrounded by its own magnificent parkland. Most Americans have a fascination with anything over a hundred years old, and Janet and I were no exception. To our delight the castle that stood in front of us was a wonderful example of the ancient threads that make up the tapestry of English history, the original having probably been built in the early fifteenth century. The ancient deer park in which it was set circled elegant gardens that looked as though they had been there forever. An ancient wisteria vine climbed three stories up the main block of the house, softening the gray stone.

I couldn't wait to see the inside and from the look on Janet's face, I wasn't alone. Her camera was out and at the ready. Andy and Emily had visited the ancient rooms many times before and so we arranged to meet them later in the gardens. As we were getting ready to pay our admission Andy took Janet to one side and whispered in her ear, "I think I should warn you, Luv. People have been known to disappear in there, never to be seen again."

Janet's eyes lit up with laughter, as she played along. "What do you mean?" she whispered back.

"Well, there have been rumors of sightings of the ghost of Sir Philip Courtney, the original owner of the castle, and then, of course, there are the hidden passages. Once a person stumbles into one of those, who knows where and when they'll get out? Anyway," he turned to me with a wink, "I advise you to keep a good eye on this young lady."

I joined in the fun and promised I'd keep my eyes peeled for any danger, especially in the dungeons, and then, with a wave, we were on our way. For a moment I looked back at the elderly couple as they walked hand in hand toward the gardens. There was something so special about them and once more, I felt grateful for having met them.

The castle lived up to its reputation and we strolled through huge rooms decorated with intricate plasterwork and handsome furnishings. Dark likenesses of stern-faced ancestors stared down at us reprovingly from ornate gilt frames. The family portraits and other paintings could have commanded my attention for hours. There was so much to see, but the time had flown and it was time to meet Andy and Emily.

"There you are," called Andy as we left the building and entered the old Victorian rose gardens. Andy and Emily led us to a bench with a view of the distant ocean where we could sit down to rest our weary feet. The abundance and variety of roses was breathtaking, and tired though she was, Janet couldn't resist taking a few more photos to share at home.

"Well, did you enjoy seeing how the other half lives?" Andy asked.

Full of enthusiasm, Janet replied, "I'll tell you something. I wouldn't mind having that Axminster carpet that was in the music room in my apartment back home. Of course, I might have to cut it down just a little, and even then it would fill the whole place, but what an exquisite piece of workmanship. And how about that clock; I believe the guide said it was fourteen feet high! But I guess that that might be a little cramped with our eight foot ceilings," she added.

"The whole place makes you feel as though you're walking through a movie," I declared. "Those carved heraldic beasts would fit into a Vincent Price movie with no problem. They and the guys in the portraits just didn't seem too happy. Maybe they didn't know about the *Three Principles*," I smiled.

"And speaking of the *Three Principles*, Andy, what you've said about *Mind* totally entrances me. Throughout the past year I've often tried to understand your paradoxical statements, wondering how it was possible for both the *Universal Mind* and our personal mind to be the same. Isn't that a contradiction?" I waited for his reply.

The gardener thought for a moment before responding, then replied, "If I were you Eric, I'd forget all about Big Mind and little mind and just call it *Mind* and I'm sure you will find it more beneficial and less confusing. After all, there is only one *Mind*."

Janet smiled at his answer although she still looked somewhat perplexed. Glancing over at her, the gardener's eyes creased in a smile as he said,

"Let not your human mind separate you
from the Universal Mind,
For they are one Mind caught up in a Divine Illusion."

Janet shifted in her seat and told the gardener that she still didn't quite understand what he was trying to tell us. "Could you define what *Universal Mind* is, in some other way?"

Andy glanced up at the wisteria vines encircling the leaded windows in the wall behind us. There was a faint humming from the roses all around us as the bees enjoyed their work. I felt I was sitting in the perfect English garden with the most unusual people. Finally he softly replied,

> *"Universal Mind is the seat of all consciousness.*
> *Universal Mind is the consciousness of all things,*
> *whether in form or formless.*
> *Universal Mind is the intelligence of all things,*
> *whether in form or formless.*
> *Universal Mind holds the secret to all*
> *psychological functioning."*

Then he looked into Janet's eyes and said, "*Universal Mind* is one of the greatest secrets known to humanity and the moment anyone starts to explain what it is, it becomes a metaphorical mystery."

Astounded, I told Andy, "I've never, ever, heard *Mind* described that way."

Janet and I looked at each other and suddenly couldn't help bursting into laughter at Andy's remarkable answer. Both the gardener and Emily sat with the most endearing smiles, ready to join the two of us in a good joke. When we finally managed to calm down, Janet, in her customary good-humored manner, told the gardener he really was "shorting her circuits" with some of his extraordinary answers.

With an intense look on his face, Andy reached over and held Janet's hand, and in a gentle, loving voice said, "I think you're trying too hard to figure it out, Luv." He then reminded us that this was one of those things that the intellect could never figure out in a million years, and asked us not to take it personally. "It's not that you're not clever," he assured us. "If you were a thousand-fold more intelligent than you are at the present moment, you still wouldn't be able to figure it out."

Rubbing her head, Janet chuckled at the gardener's words. "Andy, I'd forgotten how you talk, and I don't mean your accent either. It's your paradoxical way of expressing your philosophy."

Andy laughed and rejoined that he thought it was the way she was listening that was causing the paradox.

Janet grinned sheepishly. "Boy, I sure asked for that one!"

Taking the heat off her, I raised the question, "If such knowledge can't be intellectually understood, why did the wise ever even try to explain it?"

"Because," Andy responded, "The words of the wise are metaphorical clues that can guide us to a higher level of consciousness, which in turn bring some wisdom, that is, of course, if we can *see* or *hear* beyond their words. If you truly hear beyond their words, beyond their metaphors, you will realize that the answers did not come from them, but from deep within your own innate wisdom.

"As you are well aware, some people call such an experience an insight, or some may call it a revelation, or an awakening of something from within.

"Remember Janet,

"To look outside for the answers you seek is to dream. To look within is to awaken the wisdom that lies within."

Janet was listening intently, and she suddenly asked Andy, "Why do you think the intellect is unable to comprehend such knowledge? Yet," she added, "you say it can be understood from an insight or a revelation. What I'd like to know is, what is the difference between one and the other?"

"Janet," Andy murmured gently, "I've already explained it to you, but you failed to hear what was said. How could anyone possibly explain such a formless phenomenon? All I can tell you is, when you intellectually understand, you have obtained information from this outside world of form. On the other hand, when you have a true insight, you have tapped into your own innate wisdom, something that you had not previously realized, or let's say that you had temporarily forgotten."

I couldn't get it together. What seemed a confusing theory to me, the gardener was calmly propounding as simple fact. "Do you honestly believe that deep inside everyone's consciousness there lies an innate wisdom?"

"Yes, I do Eric. This is where *all* true knowledge exists. As therapists, you could call it a gateway to your psyche, or if you're more comfortable with another word, you could say your soul.

"Your soul and psyche are the same. Again, only the words differ. This is why many throughout time have told us to look *inside* for the answer we sought. Some mystics asked us to look *within*. All were expressing the same guidance with different words.

"I say look within because the vastness of this physical earth and sky with all its solar systems is minuscule compared to what lies within every living soul walking the face of this earth."

Janet and I looked at each other in wonder. What could the gardener possibly mean? I shook my head. "Andy, that's quite a statement."

Andy appeared to think for a minute before saying, "Intellectually finding something new in this world can be a wonderful experience and very fulfilling. Our intelligence is one of the most priceless things on this earth and we couldn't live without it.

"However, a true insight is not of this world. One could say:

> *"With our intellect, we discover.*
> *With an insight, we uncover."*

Janet and I were once again awed by Andy's answer, and I felt with certainty that we were in for another very interesting few days.

Andy told us he felt that we had had enough talk for a while and suggested we take a leisurely walk through some of the castle grounds that we had not yet covered. We circled the castle enjoying the pleasant outlooks in every direction, including a distant view of the ocean. No wonder Andy and Emily loved to come here. Janet slowly turned full circle and declared that she was enthralled by the grandeur of the place. She had scarcely finished talking, when six deer appeared from the woods and started to browse right in front of us. On the other side of the bridge, three horses grazed peacefully in a manicured meadow. We stopped nearby at a park bench shaded from the afternoon sun by an aristocratic old oak. Sitting in complete silence and witnessing such beauty, a feeling of peace and serenity swept over me. After a long silence, Janet remarked that she had never felt so relaxed in all of her life.

We continued to sit in agreeable silence for some time, enjoying the stillness, our own thoughts and the quiet company of good friends. Once again it was Janet who broke the spell, suggesting that we return to town for a late lunch. We all suddenly became aware of how hungry we were and readily agreed.

Chapter Seven
About Listening

*I*t was now Thursday and our visit to Devon and the gardener was nearing its end. Andy and Emily had invited us over to see their home, and when we arrived, I marveled at the picturesque old stone cottage with its thatched roof. Climbing roses and ivy partially covered the walls, providing a handsome backdrop to the bright spurs of delphinium, hollyhock and snapdragons that dominated the entrance garden.

As we approached the cottage, Emily appeared with a welcoming smile and invited us into her dream cottage. The living room was quite large, the polished oak floors accented with British India carpets and runners. The most striking feature was a large bay window framing a view of rolling, green meadows dotted with grazing sheep. On the left wall leading to the windows stood an oak bookcase with the rich patina attained only by age, filled with books, almanacs and periodicals. Dominating the other was a centuries-old stone fireplace with a heavy oak mantel. Janet could hardly contain her enthusiasm as Emily showed us through the house. "Oh, this is so beautiful! Wow, I love this space!" Janet exclaimed again and again as we visited each room. One wing contained a charming but very functional country kitchen with one wall almost entirely devoted to a display of trophies and pictures of Clydesdale horses.

After the tour through her home, Emily showed us outside to the patio where a table had been laid for tea and sandwiches. We sat and chatted and Janet explained to her that we were now partners in a clinic and that it had been our best year ever. Then she proudly showed Emily her engagement ring and told her that she was getting married next month, "to the most wonderful man."

Emily smiled at Janet's excitement, and offered congratulations and the hope that some day she and Andy would have the good fortune to meet him.

Janet, full of feeling, described to Emily how she sometimes couldn't believe what had happened in her life during the past twelve months. "There are times when I think I should pinch myself. It has been the most memorable year in my life. I can't believe my good fortune. Do you realize that in the past year, I've found the perfect place for my practice, with ideal partners and, as a bonus, I work with colleagues I both respect and admire? On top of that, I'm getting married to the man of my dreams."

Eyes sparkling, Emily asked Janet to tell her all about this young man of hers. Janet was happy to oblige. "Well, Jack's a very gentle person, the same age as me and I think he's very handsome. He's slightly over six feet tall, has blond, wavy hair, and big, soft, blue eyes I could just drown in," she beamed. "Jack's a pharmacist; he runs his own business and this weekend, he is opening up a second store. That's why he didn't come to England. The price you pay for success!" She sighed dramatically.

A moment later, Janet became very serious. "Emily, we're getting married at the end of October. If I were to invite you and Andy to our wedding, would you consider coming?"

"My goodness, this is a surprise. How kind of you to even think of inviting us. I'll certainly pass on the good news to Andy and tell him of your invitation. Believe me, I'm flattered that you came all this way to speak to us, and now you honor us even more by inviting us to your wedding."

"I know it's a long way to the United States, but if you could possibly make it, Jack and I would be honored to have you attend.

"Since the last time we were here in England, Eric and I have had incredible results at the office and we feel that whatever Andy said to us the last time we were here had a lot to do with it. That's why we came back to England—to ask Andy for more details about his philosophy; and I really wanted to ask you personally if you would be able to come to my wedding."

Emily sipped her tea and made no reply for a while. Finally she replied, "You must be a very proud and happy young lady."

"I am, and I feel so fortunate. I really would like to go deeper into the philosophical beliefs that both you and Andy seem to understand so clearly."

"I'm not so sure about my clarity," Emily said, smiling. "Believe me, Janet, I still sometimes have trouble relating to what Andy is saying and I would never take it upon myself to imagine I could. As long as I've known Andy, he's always had that mysterious quality of appearing to be just one step ahead of you."

"Emily, what do you mean when you say Andy often appears to be one step ahead of you?"

Emily smiled sweetly. "That my dear, I can't possibly explain to you."

"Emily, there must be some reason for you to describe your husband that way. Couldn't you have a go at explaining it to us?"

Emily sat in silence for the longest time and then said, "Since the very first time I met Andy, I could feel there was something different about him."

"In what way?" Janet inquired.

Emily appeared to be deep in thought. There was another long silence as she pondered Janet's question. Then she said, "Even when Andy was young he never said very much, but when he did, he always caught the attention of those listening. He was always very confident in what he was saying, but not in an arrogant way. Andy was always so—matter of fact."

Emily's eyes shone with love. "I knew the first night I met Andy that he was someone I wanted to share the rest of my life with."

Janet clasped her hands and nodded. "You know that I'm a marriage counsellor, Emily, so I love to hear about happy marriages, and apart from that, I'm just plain nosey." She leaned forward and pleaded earnestly, "So will you please tell me more about you and Andy?"

Emily set her cup down and sat up straighter in her chair. "Let me see if I can explain Andy. I don't know if I can, but I'll try. Not long after we were married, I started to notice that things always appeared to go right for him. At first I thought it was just sheer luck on his part, but it became more and more obvious over time that Andy knew a lot more than I was giving him credit for."

"In what way?" Janet asked, still leaning forward, not wanting to miss a word.

Emily laughed, "Janet, you have met the man and I'm sure you understand the impossible task of trying to explain Andy to anyone."

"Emily, just try! I'm dying to hear every little detail."

"He was just different from everyone else. For some reason as young as he was, he always knew exactly what crop to plant and when to sell. I remember, during the Depression days of the Thirties, that farmers all over England were having a difficult time making ends meet. Few people had any money to buy what the farmers were producing. As a matter of fact, many farmers went bankrupt and lost their farms to taxes.

"When any of our neighbors were in trouble, Andy was always one of the first to help save them and their farms. He always claimed, 'to give is to receive,' and believe me, Janet, throughout my life I've seen proof of his words a thousand times."

"That's beautiful, Emily," Janet murmured, then remarked that she had noticed all the trophies displayed in the kitchen. "What's the story behind them?"

"Those are Andy's trophies. When he was young, he specialized in breeding Clydesdale horses."

"I take it by the number of trophies that he had good horses. He must have been very successful."

"Janet, he had the most beautiful animals you have ever seen. Every one of them was a prize-winner. Andy cared for them as though they were his children. However, after the Second World War horses were gradually replaced by tractors and the Clydesdales became redundant."

"Oh, that was a shame," Janet sympathized.

"They meant a lot to him and he was able to keep his three favorites as pets," Emily said, smiling. She continued her story. "Do you know, Janet, it pleases me no end to see Andy so happy. Since we came home to the family cottage he's a different man. This is where we belong, on the farm. To us, living here is like our own little bit of heaven. I don't know if you know this or not, but Andy was born in this very cottage; we lived in it for many years. It was the main farmhouse for more than a century, until the early Fifties, in fact, when we felt the need for more space. That's when we had the new farmhouse built and moved out of the cottage."

It was obvious from Emily's joyful and vibrant demeanor that she and Andy were completely content to be living in their own little dream house again.

I commented on the beauty of their cottage. "I love your living room, it's so spacious, and the view! It's the kind of pastoral scene that makes me wish I could paint. I love the look of dormer windows, too. My wife, Norma, would fall in love with your house. I can't believe this cottage is nearly two hundred years old, Emily, it's in immaculate condition."

Emily explained that back in 1951 when they built the main house, she and Andy had had the cottage renovated, inside and out. "We were lucky; every family that ever lived here thought the cottage had a very special feeling to it, and, as you noticed, Eric, every one of them has taken wonderful care of the place.

"When Andy and I lived up in the main farm-house, nice as it was, it was always our hope to come back some day to retire to our own cottage. That's why Andy only sold half the farm and let the other half to a tenant. We never thought the renter would leave the cottage to us so soon. When we first let the farm, the renter needed it for his farm help. But as it happened, the help soon went out and bought a house of their own. So it worked out well for everyone concerned."

Just then, Andy appeared at the door leading to the garden and greeted Janet with a hug. He told us that he had been looking forward to seeing us again and hoped we were enjoying our holiday. For the next while, Emily and Andy kept us entertained with stories about the farm's history.

Then, after a short lull, I brought up a conversation that Janet and I had had during the flight over, about all of us experiencing individual truths. "We discussed the natural tendency to question and cross-question each other, to delve deeper into each other's psychological, spiritual, philosophical or political beliefs. I explained to Janet that this was why I went to India, to seek out wise people and find out what they knew. So I was wondering, Andy, have you ever met an enlightened person?"

"I'm afraid not," he replied.

"When I was in India I had the good fortune to meet quite a few enlightened individuals and some of them were very interesting," I said. "However, I'm afraid that for some reason none of their wisdom rubbed off on me, regardless of how many questions I asked."

Andy nodded his agreement. Then he replied, "If I ever did have the good fortune to meet such a person, I would most certainly want to ask questions. But, more importantly Eric, I would *listen* and savor their answers."

While I agreed with his words one hundred percent and I knew I should be listening to Andy, I was curious to know more about his philosophy. So I asked, "Andy, do you honestly believe that everyone has mental health within their own being?"

"Yes, that's the way I see it, Eric, and this inner mental health lies deep in your psyche waiting to be uncovered. It lies beyond the mental activity of personal thought. This knowledge I speak of is sometimes called 'wisdom.'"

Looking very serious, Janet asked, "Andy, am I hearing correctly? Do you believe that this knowledge and understanding lies within the psyche of everyone? If this is the case, why is it so difficult for us to retrieve it?"

"Why? Because it is hidden in a maze of personal wrong thinking. However, this I can assure you:

> *"When found, wisdom cleanses the channels*
> *of the mind*
> *and acts like a penicillin for the soul."*

Turning to me he said, "Why do you think so many of your friends in India meditated? Were they not trying to uncomplicate their minds and cast away all the unnecessary thoughts that were contaminating their thought systems?

"I'm simply telling you that such knowledge does exist and the trick is to realize that you already know."

"I don't understand what you mean," Janet interposed. "Exactly why do you say, 'We already know'?"

"Because you do," he replied.

"Is that your answer? 'Because we do'? " Janet appealed.

"Yes, that's all the answer you need—if you can *hear* beyond the metaphorical words, you just might recognize something that you have long forgotten.

"Again, I suggest that you should look for simplicity and not get caught up in a long drawn-out explanation, or you will only confuse yourself. Just *listen*."

"You mean listen to you?" I asked.

"Absolutely not. When I say you have to learn to listen, I mean you have to listen to everybody and everything. This *listening* I am referring to has nothing to do with listening to words. *Listening* is when your babbling thought system takes a rest, when it stops analysing, and listens with purity of thought.

> *"Listening is hearing from the Impersonal in absolute neutrality."*

Pointing a finger at me, he smiled and told me that I would have to stop trying to intellectually figure out his words if I wanted to understand what the wise people in India had been trying to tell me. I admitted to Andy that he was correct in his assumption that I had probably missed a lot of wisdom by not listening more intently to some of the people I'd met on my Indian tour.

Andy immediately responded, "I doubt that, Eric."

That startled me. "Why do you say that?" I asked.

"Because no matter how intently you listened, if you listened only to their words, you would have heard very little. As a matter of fact that must be precisely what you did.

"I'm afraid, young man, it just wasn't your fate to *hear* when you were in India. Perhaps you were trying too hard and filled your mind with a lot of mixed signals."

"What do you mean, 'Trying too hard'?" I asked. "I thought I was supposed to search hard?"

Andy chuckled at my question, then answered, "I guess so, if that's what you want to believe."

He didn't get into a debate with me; he didn't elaborate on his point of view nor did he try to negate mine. He just sat there and smiled. His eyes sparkled and appeared full of life as if he were trying to tell me something. But I had no idea what in heaven's name it was! This behavior was both annoying and endearing. Past experience had proved that with Andy, that certain look on his face spelt trouble. I knew he was up to something because of his disinclination to discuss whether or not one should search hard.

It seemed to me Andy was being a little too evasive, yet my curiosity was getting the better of me and I asked him, "If you had been searching in India as I was, what would you have done differently?"

"My word, Eric, that is a Golden Guinea question. To begin with, I wasn't with you in India so I have no idea what you did or didn't do during your Asian trip, except for the little you've shared with me on your visits here."

"I realize that, Andy, but use your imagination. Tell me what you would have done if you had been there."

Janet listened intently, waiting for Andy's answer.

"Are you sure you want to hear this?" Andy asked.

"Yes, I really do," I replied.

"In that case—I wouldn't have gone to India to find *Truth* because I know it's in my own backyard. But I would love some day to go to India and Nepal and experience a different culture from England.

"Do you know something, Eric? You are as close to *Truth* right this second as you ever will be. Why don't you just learn to relax and appreciate what you have in life? When you do, I guarantee that you will stand a far greater chance of finding what you are looking for than by running all over the world looking for it."

I was a little put out by his remark about my lack of readiness. I asked him why he felt that way.

"First of all, Eric, I can see that you have taken what I said personally and I wish you wouldn't. Remember I told you that such knowledge is *impersonal* and pertains to *all* human beings on earth."

"Andy, how can you be so sure that I wasn't ready to hear when I was in India?"

"Elementary, my dear Watson," he replied. "Simple logic. If you had been ready, you would have *heard* what they were trying to convey to you—the very fact that you didn't, is surely the proof!"

The way Andy put it startled me, but he was dead on target. Then he said, "I guarantee you, Eric, if you had met the wisest person on earth, you wouldn't have known it because you were thinking and listening with your own preconceived, egotistical ideas and understanding. Believe me, this is one of the biggest pitfalls to befall most searchers for such knowledge."

Dumbfounded by his words, I asked, "How can anybody possibly seek without thinking with his own ideas and concepts?"

"Just be," he replied.

Janet shook her head from side to side signifying her bewilderment. "That's seems like an impossible task. How do we accomplish it? What do you mean, 'Just be'?"

"My advice is: Still your mind until you reach the state of *no thought*. If you do, you will find many of the answers you seek."

I couldn't believe what I was hearing and sat there totally speechless, once again struck dumb by what seemed to me to be another of Andy's outrageous statements.

"What do you mean, the state of '*no thought*'?" Janet asked.

He replied, "The state of *no thought* is when the personal thought system finds perfect stillness, transcending time, space, and matter and finds the true nature of *Mind*."

"Andy," I asked, "what would you say is the true nature of *Mind*?"

Without any hesitation, he replied, "You haven't been listening to me. Haven't I already told you many times before?

"Mind is the universal intelligence of all things, whether in form or formless."

Andy smiled gently at my obvious consternation, "What say we get ourselves round these sandwiches and sweets, then take a stroll and forget all about *Mind*, *Consciousness* and *Thought*? You never know, we may even discover a state of no thought!" he chuckled.

Chapter Eight
What Is Truth?

*T*he following day was glorious, the weather was lovely and sunny with temperatures just over seventy degrees and we asked Andy and Emily to join us for afternoon tea at the highly recommended Silver Nutmeg Teahouse. We arrived a little early and, to our delight, discovered it was a quaint old Tudor-style house that had been converted into a restaurant. A young lady dressed in a maid's costume showed us to our table. We were pleasantly surprised to find that the table reserved for us was in a very elegant glass solarium. Between scattered British India rugs, clean, dark marble tiles glistened. Outside, there was a stunning display of shrubs and other plants surrounding a courtyard where a mermaid fountain played in a small pool. The yard attracted numerous little birds that flew in and out of the surrounding bushes.

Janet and I sat enjoying the beauty and relishing the atmosphere of the place. Suddenly, I was shaken with an overwhelming longing for Norma. I knew how much she would have enjoyed the experience of high tea in England with such delightful hosts and I wished I could share it with her. We ordered a drink while waiting for Andy and Emily to arrive and discussed our earlier talks with the gardener, how many of his answers seemed somewhat ambiguous and difficult to understand. "As far as I'm concerned, I'm picking up more of a feeling than an understanding," I admitted.

"I know what you mean, Eric. When I listen to Andy, it's more of a good feeling than anything else. As a matter of fact, when I arrived home last night, his words started to come alive, and to a degree, I got an inkling of what he was talking about, but then it would vanish and I couldn't remember one word he'd said."

"That's exactly what happened to me," I responded. "But it was also as if I had come to my senses all of a sudden, and realized something deeper and more profound about how our thoughts really do have a direct tie with our behavior—and then I would start to wonder why I didn't see this before."

This conversation somehow made Janet and I laugh so hard that the tears streamed down our faces. Finally, after we had exhausted our fit of laughter and regained our composure, Janet said, "You have to admit, Eric, this is really weird. Here we are, two professionals who have travelled all the way from the

United States, sitting in an English teahouse waiting for a gardener to tell us something that will enhance our knowledge of our own profession."

The very thought of it sent both of us into peals of laughter again. Each time we regained control, our mirth would burst out again; the merest glance would send either Janet or me into another paroxysm of merriment until we sat exhausted and helpless. Finally we calmed down sufficiently to continue the discussion we had been having on the plane regarding our separate beliefs. We wondered if there was such a thing as one truth, as many sages and mystics throughout the ages have believed.

After some further deliberation we came to the conclusion that what is considered truth can vary from person to person, and therefore, there can't possibly be only one truth.

"Of course," I declared knowledgeably, "this is why we should accept each other's opinions and beliefs without getting too upset or too opinionated."

"Most definitely," Janet agreed. "I accept what you envision as your truth and, as you just said, Eric, you respect mine, regardless of the fact that we know we will differ in our beliefs and opinions from time to time.

"Imagine being so stubborn that you believed that your truth was the only truth that existed? No doubt, such a person would have quite a few problems in his or her life. I guess you and I have seen many people in our lives who fitted that category and everyone of them was very unhappy."

"When you think about it, Janet, if everybody's truth is true to them, how can there possibly be such a thing as one truth?"

"There can't possibly be such a thing," Janet nodded. "After all, it's inevitable that we will differ in our opinions from time to time. It's only natural that we will have varying beliefs and concepts regarding life. For example, religion, politics and education are but a few of the thousands of subjects we could disagree on."

We continued to discuss the subject of truth until finally Andy and Emily appeared. Emily greeted us warmly, then inquired if we had eaten yet.

"Not yet. We were waiting for you and having a good discussion. Would you like a cup of tea?" I asked.

"I'd love a cup of tea," answered Emily, "and I'm sure Andy will have one, too."

Janet remarked how old fashioned and charming the teahouse was. "The waitress told me it was over three hundred years old. What amazes me is the wooden beams that hold up the whole structure. They're so old, they're almost coal black. I find it hard to believe they're still here after all this time, still functioning, and they're so beautiful," she enthused.

We couldn't resist ordering the Devonshire cream tea that was being served, fluffy scones piled high with rich clotted cream and home-made strawberry jam. "This is totally decadent. I'll never be able to fit into my wedding dress if I keep this up," Janet wailed. "I just hope Jack will recognize me when I get off the plane. Oh, well, as you say, Emily, 'In for a penny, in for a pound.' And I mean that literally," she giggled as she reached for another dab of the delicious cream.

"It's alright," Emily said, laughing sympathetically, "this is a very special variety that has absolutely no calories. You can eat as much as you want with no bad consequences."

"What a relief," Janet mumbled with her mouth full. "Now I definitely know I've died and gone to heaven."

We all concentrated on enjoying our meal until there was little left on the tea table but crumbs and crusts. Then I started to tell Andy and Emily how Janet and I had had a good discussion on truth and how the two of us had come to the conclusion that there was no such thing as one truth and we most definitely agreed that everybody has their own interpretation of what truth is.

Andy and Emily glanced at each other and Emily, elegantly holding her cup of tea, replied, "That's a very interesting way to look at it Eric, and

I'm certain you are correct in what you just said about everyone's personal truth." Then with a very serious look on her face, she said, "I'm just afraid that as people start to change their minds more readily, then there will be goodness knows how many new truths in this world and that could get very confusing. After all, how many people live on this planet?"

"I believe it's over four billion people," I answered, "and that's a lot of individual truths." Andy was grinning from ear to ear. Suddenly, I had the strangest feeling that Emily was up to something and I had just been drawn into a trap.

Janet took the bait and continued to explain how many truths were in China alone.

Emily immediately responded, "China, that's a country with a tremendous population, changing their personal truths every day."

At this point, Andy dropped his head and put his hand over his mouth to stop himself from laughing out loud. Janet caught on that something was going on, grinned and asked, "What are you guys laughing at?"

Andy, with a gentle smile, remarked, "I'm afraid I have to disagree with you, Luv, and stand firm in my belief that there is only *One Truth*. And when I say only *One Truth* I'm not talking about anyone's personal truth."

Janet grinned at Andy's reply, saying, "Okay, Andy, I'll bite. How can there be only *One Truth*?"

"Janet, please allow me to answer you in an indirect way. First, we have what we call our personal truth and our personal truth is what we believe to be true or false in this physical reality we live in. As you already know, our personal truths can change from moment to moment depending on the circumstances of our life.

"However, there's a greater *Truth* that is Impersonal and is spiritual in nature. This *Truth* is unchangeable, unexplainable, and unnameable.

"The trick is, you have to go beyond personal truth to a greater *Spiritual Truth* that lies deep within your own psyche."

To say the least, his answer took Janet and me by surprise. "Andy," I said, "that's an extraordinary answer. Would you please clarify it for us? Why do you feel there's a difference between personal truth and what you're calling *Spiritual Truth*?"

"Because, Eric, *Spiritual Truth* is *Impersonal* and is not of this world. Such truth lies beyond time, space and matter and is unchangeable."

Then smiling broadly he said, "On the other hand, our personal truth can change from moment to moment and is subject to what I would call psychological viruses."

Andy's words again caught me by surprise, yet they certainly stimulated my curiosity. I had never heard any therapist talk about such things as psychological viruses. For that matter I couldn't recall anyone at all ever mentioning the term, except maybe for Andy, who had talked briefly about them the last time I was in England.

"What do you mean by 'psychological virus'?" I inquired.

"Before I answer that question Eric, I hope you understand that I'm not talking to you as a therapist; I'm talking about *every* human being on earth, immaterial of what their stature or vocation might be.

"Now, please remember, once again I am speaking from an impersonal point of view, which is neutral and judges nobody. So don't take it personally if some of my philosophical views on life differ with some of your beliefs or training.

"What I am calling psychological viruses would be such things as greed, hate, jealousy, desire and envy, just to name a few. Such viral thoughts create negative feelings and lead to insurmountable problems for those who are infected. Believe me, everyone in this world is subject to such viruses; they can even be transmitted. So before you start putting labels on people, try to understand such viruses are as natural as breathing and nobody journeys through this life completely immune from them.

"When you are suffering from such a virus you are not sick per se. I would rather say you are temporarily and *innocently* not thinking straight."

"Why do you call them viruses?" Janet inquired.

"Because they create negative feelings and mindsets that rob us of our sanity and inner peace and disallow us peace of mind."

I really didn't know how to respond to his words. After the longest time, I asked Andy if he would explain to us more about his philosophy of what he was calling "psychological viruses."

Andy took a sip of his tea, and then said, "What I am calling psychological viruses can come in many strains. They can all create an enormous amount of *unnecessary* negative feelings and needless suffering for many a poor soul on this earth."

Without really thinking, I inquired, "How many strains do you figure there are?"

"Too many to mention," he replied with a laugh.

"I feel quite silly even asking such a question, Andy," Janet said, "but in your opinion is there any immunization or remedy for these so-called psychological viruses?"

Andy took a deep breath, gradually exhaled, then without further hesitation replied, "The secret vaccine for such psychological viruses lies in your *thoughts* and your *feelings*. Feelings such as love, caring, sharing or being pleased by the good fortune enjoyed by yourself or others are just a few of the remedies that can lift your spirit and clear away the unwanted viruses of negative feelings."

"But why do you call negative thoughts and feelings viruses?" Janet persisted.

"Because, Janet," Andy answered, "negative thoughts and feelings contaminate the human soul and spread mental imbalance, bringing to the owner a clouded version of reality which he can spread to others. For example, if someone is suffering from such viruses as greed, hate, vengeful feelings, jealousy, envy or insecurity, that person can never find peace of mind. Peace of mind will not come about until he truly sees that it's his own thoughts that are, innocently, creating his problems—and I repeat, innocently."

"I notice that you speak about feelings a lot," Janet remarked. "Why do you put so much emphasis on feelings?"

"Yes, Luv, I do. Because our feelings are one of the most important things in our lives.

"Our feelings are the barometer of the soul.
They are the measure of our thinking.
They let us know what mental weather we can expect;
They let us know how we are faring in life."

"Andy, what about people who have anxiety attacks? What if it's in the genes as some are supposing?"

"I have no idea how to answer that question, Janet. After all I'm not a therapist or a geneticist. But if I, personally, were depressed or overanxious, I'd look at my thoughts and recognize that they were the source of my feelings; then I'd try to change those upsetting thoughts as soon as possible. Believe me, genes cannot have anything to do with *Mind,* as I told you before. *Mind* is by nature spiritual and has no form of its own, therefore it can't possibly be carried in a gene."

"You know, Andy," continued Janet, "it's pretty common for medical students to think they have many of the diseases they are studying—sort of a disease of the week. Well, that was me as a Psychology graduate student. I don't know if you know this or not Andy, but as Psychology students we never studied health. We only studied diseases, and like many others I began to recognize, in myself, all the symptoms I was reading about and fell into moments of anxiety and depression.

"As I became more and more obsessed with these symptoms they appeared to grow stronger and I saw myself as a clinically depressed person and a clinically anxious person. I just didn't know that it is perfectly natural to have low thoughts and thoughts of insecurity that would pass uneventfully if they were seen for what they were.

"It was no wonder many senior psychology students took more medication and thought they needed more therapy than they had as freshmen. I'm just this minute starting to realize that my problem wasn't just the stress of school, as I thought at the time; it was my pessimistic focus on mental sickness.

"When I believed I had these illnesses, the more that unconstructive focus brought credibility to my thoughts, the more the illnesses became a reality."

Andy had been listening attentively to Janet's recollections but then he broke in. "It really doesn't surprise me that your obsession with your symptoms lent credibility to your thinking you were ill," he said, but I am amazed to hear that you didn't receive any tuition on mental health. Why do you suppose that was?"

"I have no idea," Janet replied. "It's astonishing, isn't it? All I know is my entire instruction concentrated on behavior and past traumas leading to mental illness."

I then described to Andy how we were taught that genetics and childhood conditioning were the bogie men that smote us with the scourge of mental illness. "When I graduated I felt powerless and hopeless and governed by powers beyond my control. The trouble was that what we were taught in school about illness continued to color my practice. I can only talk for myself, but I remember that at first I had no idea what to do with a client who was in good spirits. I wasn't prepared for that. I wanted to deal with illness and in all innocence, I often tried to lead them into a situation by bringing up problems from their past. Quite often I warned them not to be overly positive or they might set themselves up for disappointment. I realize now that I was denying myself and everyone else hope."

Janet dropped her head in mock shame, then gave an embarrassed chuckle. "Let me tell you a story. Sometime after my first meeting you, Andy, a good friend of mine heard about the success I was having in my practice. He suggested that we might go into practice together and, to that end, that I should visit him in his new office someday.

"When I went to visit him I found it next to impossible to find a parking spot, which I found very frustrating. I thought to myself, 'What a crazy place to open a new clinic, there's so little parking for his clients.' After circling round the area half a dozen times I finally found a parking spot quite a distance from the clinic.

"Of course I was late for our meeting, and when I entered my friend's office, I told him about the trouble I had finding a place to park and said it must be very annoying and frustrating for his clients, adding to their distress before coming to their session. He laughed at me and said, 'Janet, that's the idea. As you know I am a psychoanalytic therapist and the frustration the clients vent on me is called transference; and as you also know, transference is a good thing because it gives me some illness to work on.'

"I told him I no longer believed in using transference as a therapeutic tool and that now I do the very opposite. Now, I want my clients to be as comfortable and high spirited as possible during their session. He seemed really surprised, and asked me why I would want them to be in high spirits when I saw them.

"I then explained to him that it's because I want to bring out their own mental health, not their mental stress. 'Surely this is why they are coming to us,' I told him, 'to find some peace of mind and, if possible, their mental health. So why would I want to get them all angry and frustrated when they arrive in my office?'

"That man had absolutely no idea what I was talking about, and he accused me of being unrealistic and never again asked me to join his practice."

When Andy heard Janet's story he howled with laughter and asked Janet if she was pulling his leg.

"No, I'm dead serious. Honestly, Andy, that is a true story and to this day that man still practices that way. I tried to tell him that I now know that frustration is bad for both the client and the therapist and that I prefer to join my clients in a world of well being and even laughter.

"I must say, I was surprised to see that it made him so furious," Janet continued. "He lost his cool and yelled at me that he was taught at school, just as I was, that a serious and uncomfortable emotional environment was the appropriate therapeutic milieu and that Freud said that humor is just an expression of anger.

"I tried to calm him by saying that surely he could see that such ideas are humorous and hold no common sense whatever. That's when he became enraged. I knew my friend was not a very happy soul, but I had never seen him behave as he did then. He was so disturbed by his perception that I was trying to put down his techniques.

"I apologized, trying to let him know that I had not intended to offend or upset him but I could see that he wanted nothing to do with my ideas.

"Driving home after our meeting I couldn't comprehend my friend's negative reaction to what I had said and I kept asking myself what I had said that made him so upset. Surely it wasn't because I mentioned that I like to get my clients into a more positive mood? I found it difficult to believe that this same man had asked me to join him in his practice because of the successful results I was getting."

"This I can guarantee you, Janet. When the time comes and therapists like your friend start to see the connection between the *Three Principles* and our psychological nature, it will be a blessing to them and they will see a deeper dimension of their profession than they ever imagined."

Andy's assuredness took me aback for a few seconds as it often did, then I realized he was not just saying these words; he meant every one of them. Then I told him, "Up until the day I met you, Andy, all mental illnesses looked terminal to me. Every day I went to my office I thought I was fighting a losing battle, but after I met you my life and my practice changed dramatically. When I saw the power we all possess to reverse our thinking to a healthy, natural thought process, I breathed a sigh of relief, knowing why I had gone into psychology in the first place."

Andy just sat without moving, without speaking, and I could see his eyes begin to well up as my words of thanks stirred something within him.

Janet remarked, "I'm with you, Eric, the seriousness and mental distress that used to be present in my office perpetuated the illness I was trying to cure. At some point after my visit to England, I realized that seriousness and discomfort is to mental illness as dark and damp is to fungus. On the other hand, love and light-heartedness are to mental illness as sunlight and dryness is to fungus. They assist to eradicate mental illness and promote mental health."

"You're right, Janet," I agreed. "What you just said makes me realize the importance of my own personal mental health. In good shape, it helps produce the dry and sunny climate where mental health thrives. What a great gift to give to anyone!"

Andy quietly listened to us share our beliefs, then when we stopped for a moment, said, "I can see that both of you now have a much greater and deeper understanding of how the *Three Principles* work and have become not only two very loving people, but also two very wise people."

His kind words touched me and gave me the courage to ask something I'd wondered about for a long time. "Tell me Andy, which of the *Three Principles* is the most important?"

"I told you before all three are equally important," he replied. "You can't have one without the other. Let me try another way to explain to you how they function. This time I will call them *Universal Principles*.

"*Universal Mind* is the intelligence of *all* things, whether in form or formless.

"*Universal Consciousness* is a gift that enables us to observe and experience the existence and workings of this world we live in.

"*Universal Thought* is also a gift that allows us to think our way through this cosmic drama.

"All *Three Principles* are spiritual by nature, therefore they have no form. That is why all three are intangible—indefinable in intellectual terms—and have to be expressed metaphorically."

Our faces reflected our struggle to understand everything that the gardener was saying, and after a short pause, Andy advised, "Don't try to analyze my words too much or you'll soon find yourselves on a wild goose chase!

"I'll tell you something, one of the most beautiful things that any human being can realize is the mystical bridge between the form and the formless. *Thought* is that bridge."

Once again I felt extremely energized. Every part of my body felt alive and the more Andy spoke the greater the feeling became. I was hearing him at a deeper level than I had experienced before. Then I wondered to myself, *Is Andy talking differently, or am I hearing him differently?*

Suddenly I realized there was a lot deeper meaning to Andy's philosophy of the principles than I had previously thought. I told him that I would love to learn more about their workings.

Andy nodded sympathetically and expressed his admiration that Janet and I had traveled so many miles just to be here. "As I sit looking at you young people, I see two therapists who have lots of love and caring in their hearts. It would be my pleasure and honor to share what little knowledge I have, but, I repeat, my knowledge is very limited. However, you have asked me and with complete neutrality I would suggest that what you should be looking for is the logic of the psyche."

Andy's words, though quite explicit, still left lots of room for the imagination. Just then the waitress came with the bill and after just one more sip of the strong tea that the English love so much, Emily suggested that since it was such a beautiful day, we could take a stroll down by the ocean.

Chapter Nine
Consciousness and Wisdom

We walked to a small park overlooking the ocean and when we came to a grassy mound, sat for a while in silence, admiring the sparkling seascape before us.

After some time had elapsed Janet remarked, "I'm not surprised that Torquay is called the Riviera of England, although at first I was amazed when I saw so many palm trees. As a matter of fact, I never thought of England as having palm trees."

I confessed that the only reason I knew about them was that I had seen them in a travel brochure.

Janet was delighted. "It truly does look like the pictures I've seen of the French Riviera," she said.

I had seldom felt such contentment, and mentioned to the others that I was very aware of how precious this time was. We all continued to reflect gratefully on our personal circumstances as we enjoyed the beauty of our surroundings. As time passed my thoughts returned to what Andy had said regarding *Consciousness*. I knew that there was more to what he was saying than meets the eye, although for the world of me, I couldn't put my finger on what it was. I was a little embarrassed that I still didn't fully comprehend, but I asked Andy once again if he would mind talking more about *Consciousness*. He bowed his head for a moment and then answered, "The gift of *Consciousness* combined with *Mind* and *Thought* allows us to experience life at an infinite number of levels of understanding. Each individual person surveys life according to his or her personal level of consciousness."

I was puzzled and I asked him, "But if we all work through the same *Three Principles*, why is it that we all see separate realities?"

"Because we all have what is called a free will, and the freedom of thought that allows us to see life as individuals. This is why the *Three Principles*, combined with our free will, create what many of the mystics throughout time have called separate realities, because we all live in our own personal cosmic drama."

"Andy," I pointed out, "what you say sometimes sounds too simplistic. I'm afraid many would say your theories are unprovable and dismiss them as just some crazy idea."

Andy looked at me and with a slight wave of his hand said, "Personally I don't care what they think or what they believe. I ask neither you nor anyone else on this earth to believe me. But more importantly, I ask you to look within yourself for the psychological answers you seek. It is here you will unravel the puzzle to all human behavior."

"Why do you say that this knowledge lies *within,* and what does within really mean?" I asked.

"My dear Eric, I have already explained to you how it is impossible for anyone to answer such a question directly. But, I can tell you that 'within' is a metaphor; within has nothing whatsoever to do with your body. Within is beyond the realm of this physical reality that you now live in.

"You know, Eric, perhaps some day you may have the good fortune to realize on your own, bit by bit, or all in a flash, what within really means. Then you will find out for yourself just how impossible a task it is to explain what it means.

"As a matter of fact, both of you have already looked within and failed to see the connection to what you call an insight and looking within."

Janet, puzzled, asked, "What do you mean when you say that both of us have already looked within?"

Spreading his hands in a gesture of frustration he asked Janet, "Where do you think all this newness in your personal and professional life is coming from?"

"Well of course, Andy, some of the credit must go to you for telling us about the principles," she answered.

"Nonsense, I only told you about them. You had the courage to look within and jump the boundaries of time—to see for yourself. In more simple terms, you have jumped ahead of your time."

As he spoke, Andy had become more animated, then forming a tent with his fingertips and raising it toward his chin, he said, "What would you say if I told you both that you have discovered something just as important for your own profession as Einstein did when he realized something that changed the science of physics for ever?"

Janet and I couldn't believe our ears and thought that Andy had gone a bit too far. His last statement struck us as outrageous exaggeration.

He stared sternly at me. "Why do you think you are having such a difficult time trying to explain all this newness to some of your old associates? What is it that is helping you in your life and in your work?"

As most of his statements did, his questions took me off guard for a few seconds, then I heard myself answering, "I guess it's because we are using the principles as well as we can."

Then it hit me like a ton of bricks. Perhaps we had found something of value, maybe not quite as spectacular as Einstein's discovery, but at least something that could well help a lot of people. But it was frustrating that neither Janet nor I knew very much about how it all works. I asked, "Andy, why is it that my friends Tom and Peter heard you and Emily just as we did and they just didn't get the connection between their thoughts and their actions? I still can't understand why they can't recognize plain common sense."

Andy raised his hand and pointing a finger at Janet, then at me, said, "Please listen to me carefully. Your friends Tom and Peter did not hear a word I was saying because they were concentrating on my words with their intellect, trying to meld whatever they knew with what I was saying, whereas you heard beyond my words to another dimension and found new knowledge to assist you through life.

"At the moment I'm afraid Tom and Peter have their own way of searching for whatever they think they are looking for. I can tell you, though, at the present moment the thought of three principle elements is rather frightening to them."

"Why do you call them elements, Andy?" Janet asked.

"For the simple reason that like any other element, they cannot be broken down into lesser components. All three are spiritual gifts that lie before time, space and matter, and we are all blessed with the ability to use these gifts as we choose, foolishly or wisely."

Janet asked Andy to give us an example. He thought for a short while, then replied. "You know how in chemistry it takes two or more elements to create a compound?"

"Yes," Janet replied, "but what has that got to do with the *Three Principles*?"

"Look at it like this Janet. *Mind, Consciousness* and *Thought* are spiritual elements that when mixed together create what I would call psychological compounds."

Janet looked to be just as surprised by his words as I was, but she forged on. "OK, Andy. What is a psychological compound?"

Andy smiled at Janet's persistence and replied, "What I am calling a psychological compound is literally anything that the human mind can conceive."

It was difficult for me to believe what the old gardener was saying and I felt I needed more time to try to comprehend his far-out philosophical beliefs. I knew deep in my gut that he was trying to tell me something important but it was certainly eluding me at the moment. Yet it was exciting to think we really may have discovered something to help in our work.

"Andy, please be patient with me—and try again, would you explain the *Three Principles* in another way? And could you tell me one more time why you place so much importance on them?"

"Eric, I can't emphasize enough the importance of the *Three Principles*. These *Three Principles* contain the foundation of all human experience here on earth. Literally, they are the three cosmic elements that we use to create our entire reality here on earth."

To me, his answer was spellbinding. I had absolutely no way to reply to such a statement so I said nothing. After a lengthy silence, Andy said, "Never forget that we human beings are thinking creatures who think our way through life every second of every day. We walk through life as thinking creatures with our thoughts painting a picture of the world we live in."

Neither of us knew how to react. Janet nodded her agreement when I said, "Andy, I find your concepts and ideas incredible."

"Eric, I want you to know that what I say is not a belief or a concept but an elemental fact that is beyond a belief or a concept. What I say to you is before the contamination of human thought and comes from another dimension of *Thought* altogether."

I was astounded by what I thought to be an outlandish answer. Janet looked over at me and rolled her eyes, indicating that she too was mystified by Andy's statement.

Andy just sat there in silence as if he were waiting for Janet or me to reply to what he had just said. Janet continued to roll her eyes dramatically and exclaimed, "Wow, Andy you're blowing my mind again."

After a long silence I told him I still didn't follow his logic regarding what he was calling psychological compounds. "I hate to ask you again but I wonder if you could elaborate a little more? Would you explain how the principles can possibly relate to some of the issues we face on a day-to-day basis?"

"All I can do, Eric, is repeat, literally anything that the human mind can conceive of, is a psychological compound.

"I'm sure you can see the negative results of mixing the *Three Principles* together to create compounds such as greed, hate, jealousy, insecurity or fear. With such feelings you are going to suffer and live in mental torment.

"Now, I ask you to mix the three elements differently and create feelings of love, happiness, contentment, caring and empathy for others. These are but a few of the positive compounds that will help bring you peace of mind."

Janet couldn't resist asking Andy to explain such a phenomenon. Tilting his head and looking down his nose as if he were wearing spectacles, he asked sternly, "Janet, are all therapists born to question and cross-question?" Then he added jokingly, "I had always thought that was a lawyer's job.

"Let me try to explain it this way. Your thoughts create your perception of the world you live in. Let's use an example. Suppose a person had a problem being too ambitious or greedy and these ambitions were creating a lot of stress in the work environment, then spilling over into family life. Then, suddenly one day, that person *realized* that his or her over-ambitious and greedy egotistical desires were the biggest creator of these problems. Such an insight would allow that person to see that he or she was missing a lot in life. This insight would be the stepping-stone to finding his or her long-lost happiness and contentment."

"How do you make such a change?" Janet asked.

"I just told you, by mixing the three psychological elements *Mind*, *Consciousness* and *Thought* differently. In short, you simply change your mind regarding how you see life. Remember, this is a world governed by thought, and when you change your thoughts, your reality changes accordingly. This you could call the logic of the psyche."

Janet looked extremely serious for a moment, and then said, "Correct me if I'm wrong, but what I hear you say is that we all constantly create compounds in our heads by merely thinking about any subject."

"That is exactly right, Janet. As a matter if fact, we are all mixing the elements right now to converse with each other."

"So what I'm hearing you say is that every time we change our minds and our thoughts we are automatically creating psychological compounds?

Is that right?" Janet continued. "What you are calling psychological compounds are ideas, beliefs or concepts?"

"Correct!" replied Andy.

"Wouldn't it be the same with our feelings of anger, love, caring?" she asked.

"Exactly," replied Andy.

I'd seldom seen Janet so excited, and whatever she was understanding was having an unbelievable effect on her. I was shocked by the sudden realization that Janet was understanding more of what Andy was saying about psychological compounds than I was. What he was saying was very foreign to my way of thinking and training, but still the gardener's unique theories were stirring something inside me.

"Andy," I asked, "what is the difference between simply changing our thoughts, like many of the popular therapeutic practices such as positive thinking or affirmations propose, and what you are referring to."

"Let's put it this way, Eric. If you simply replace one thought with another, it will only provide temporary relief. On the other hand, when you start to find the true nature of *Thought*, it will take you to a deeper level of understanding, which helps create a more permanent, deeper, healthier outlook on life—because you are finding your own inner wisdom.

"This, my friend, I can tell you:

"It is through Universal Mind, Universal Thought
and Universal Consciousness that we transform
the invisible spiritual energy into our personal reality."

For a long time not a word was said, as Janet and I tried to digest Andy's unusual answers. Finally Janet broke the silence. "Andy, what would you say is the greatest difference between your philosophical beliefs and ours?"

"That's quite the loaded question, Luv. Remember, I'm not a therapist, nor do I know much about what you believe or disbelieve. I only know what I know."

"Oh, come on, Andy, you must have some opinion on how we differ."

He looked over at Emily and she nodded at him. Andy shrugged as if to say, "Here goes," then said, "The way I see it, one of the greatest differences is that you are apt to concentrate your efforts on the defects of yourselves and others to try to fix a problem. Now please remember, I can only speak for myself. As I said before, you are the therapists, not me, and please try and remember that you are talking a completely different ideology than I."

Janet and I assured Andy that we would take no offence at his answer and would love to hear what he had to say. "After all, that's why we came all this way to visit you."

Andy lowered his head shyly as he gathered his thoughts, then straightened and said, "If I were trying to help a neighbor, I would listen to his or her story very carefully and have lots of love for the individual and empathy for his state of mind and his suffering.

"But more importantly, I would try to show my neighbor that beyond wrongful thinking exists a whole and healthy inside."

"You really do believe that there is an innate wisdom that lies inside everyone, don't you?" Janet queried.

"Yes I do, Janet. That's why I am asking you to look at your own inner strengths, not your weaknesses. If you don't, you will never allow yourself to see the innocent person that stands in front of you, *before* the lostness took place. And just beyond that lostness lies a happy, mentally healthy and wise person lost in a maze of wrongful thoughts."

His words really caught my attention and I asked Andy what he meant by "before the lostness took place."

"Believe me, Eric, from the moment of birth everybody on earth is lost to one extent or another—without exception. This is why nobody is perfect in this world of form."

"But what makes you say we are all lost at birth?" Janet asked in a shocked voice.

"Because," Andy replied, "at birth we have entered a world of form and, being newborn babes full of innocence, we lose our true spiritual identity. We have entered into our secondary home called the physical world.

"It's the most natural thing in this world to be lost, to one degree or another. However, as you are well aware, there are many degrees of lostness for a human being. Regardless of how the mind of humanity is lost or what behavioral pattern this mental lostness may take, it all derives from the wrongful usage of the *Three Principles*."

"But, Andy, the circumstances and experiences of someone's past must surely have something to do with his behavior?"

Andy raised his hand letting me know in no uncertain terms that the psychology he was talking about and what I was talking about was as night is to day. "What I'm trying to convey to you, Eric, is totally different. You concentrate on behavior and I am suggesting to you that you should look at the strength and the health of someone *before* that lost behavior was created."

"How are we supposed to do that?" I asked. "Don't you know that there are millions of ways that can lead to someone having a psychological problem? What you are asking is impossible."

"I agree with you," Andy replied, "it would be next to impossible to address the specific cause for each of so many behavioral patterns. This is why I say to you, 'Instead of concentrating on the outside behavior so much, look *inside*—before the anguish started—where the *Mind* is purer.' Never forget, *all* psychological experience here on earth derives from usage of the *Three Principles* of:

> *"Universal Mind,*
> *Universal Consciousness and*
> *Universal Thought.*

"They are the three pearls of wisdom that will take you to the knowledge that you seek."

"The trouble is, where do you find these elusive answers?" Janet said, frowning.

"To start with, Janet, if I were you, I'd forget all about trying to figure out what consciousness is, or isn't, and just use it. Today, maybe we could talk about feelings and how our thoughts play a very important role in the quality of our lives. For example, if you have feelings of jealousy, anger, sorrow and insecurity, then you are living with a negative mind-set that will rob you of your happiness and will never allow you peace of mind.

"On the other hand, if you have positive feelings such as love, contentment, gratefulness, caring for others, then you will find your peace of mind. Again, I'd like to remind you of the wise old saying,

"As you sow, so shall ye reap.

"You would be very wise to remember: Never do anything to another soul that you yourself wouldn't want them to do to you, otherwise, you will suffer the consequences of your action. I believe some people call this 'karma.'"

That rang a bell, and I said, "When I was traveling in India and the Himalayas, the people talked a considerable amount about karma, but I never really understood what they were getting at, or how karma works. Andy, why do you think some people have good karma and others have bad karma?"

"Because," he replied, "to hurt another is to hurt yourself. This is the law of karma. Never forget, sometimes the legacy of your actions may be suffering, not only for you but also for others.

"You must remember, we are all created from the same formless energy. Therefore, what you do to one, you do to the world, and bad thoughts and bad acts always return to their rightful owners like a boomerang."

"Is it possible to change bad karma into good karma or are we stuck with our bad karma for the rest of our life?" I asked.

Andy laughed at my question. "No, we are not stuck with bad karma. If you want to change it, all you have to do is change your negative habits to positive, and find some positive feelings such as love, caring, sharing. Hurt no other soul on earth. Know in your heart that you will never again do wrong to another human being. Then your karma will change to suit your thoughts and deeds. Believe me, Eric, karma is just like the ego, it is self-inflicted.

"Remember, my friends, they are *your* feelings and as I explained to you before,

"Our thoughts are the psychological threads
That weave our entire experience here on earth.
Weave your thoughts with love and respect
for your fellow man
And you will weave a blanket of love and
understanding for everyone."

Neither Janet nor I said a word. In my state of bemusement the silence that ensued seemed endless and immeasurable. My head was spinning as I tried in vain to understand what the gardener was getting at. But the more I tried to figure out what Andy was telling us, the more confused I became.

My mystification must have been very apparent because Andy looked me straight in the eyes and assured me,

"In simplicity lies the answers to all complexity."

Once again his answer took me completely off guard and I asked him if he ever spoke in plain English.

Andy laughed at my question, then became very serious. "Please listen very carefully," he said. "What is already known to us, usually appears quite simple. What is unknown to us, often appears complicated until it is known; then it becomes simple. Again, I ask you to look for simplicity and forget the already known."

Andy smiled at the look on our faces, and then gently remarked,

"When the answers are complicated, it's the Intellect. When the answers are simple, it's the Spirit."

After reflecting on Andy's latest assertions for some time, Janet steered the discussion into a new course, asking, "Andy, what, in your opinion, is our true identity?"

"That, Janet, you will have to figure out for yourself. The true seers of this world often said it was a secret they couldn't give away. Now, when they said they couldn't give it away, they didn't mean that they didn't want to give it away, or that they shouldn't give it away. On the contrary, I'm sure they would have loved to share their knowledge with the entire world. However, they were wise enough to know that such knowledge was formless, hence indecipherable to the human intellect and intangible to our five senses. They knew that their words alone couldn't explain the secret they carried in their hearts. This is why I say to you, one of the main things to remember is this:

"True wisdom is not discovered, but uncovered
from an uncontaminated innate intelligence.
Wisdom lies beyond our delusionary ego
and personal thought system.
Believe me, words do not convey the magnificence
of the hidden treasures that lie within.

"This I can tell you. When the listener isn't ready to hear such knowledge, that person will hear what sounds like foolishness and nonsense, just as your friends Tom and Peter did."

His answer appeared to go well beyond answering Janet's question, yet it intrigued me, so I said, "I was always taught that wisdom came with age so I've rather been looking forward to becoming a senior citizen."

With a little chuckle, Andy assured me, "It's unfortunate for you then, Eric, but the idea that wisdom has anything to do with age is a fallacy. A small child can be wiser than the oldest person alive. What you have to realize is that obtaining wisdom and obtaining experience in life are like apples and oranges; they differ significantly.

"Many go through life and accumulate a lot of experience, but accrue little or no wisdom. Others, even in a short life accumulate much wisdom."

"Your idea of wisdom and mine must be quite different, Andy. What does the word mean to you?" Janet asked.

Andy pondered her question for a little while before replying, "To me, wisdom is a spiritual intelligence before the contamination of human thought. When found, it helps clear our personal minds of ignorance and misunderstanding. This, in turn, helps clean our psyches and creates a beautiful working reality."

Janet caught her breath at the gardener's words. "Wow! That's quite a mouthful."

"Are you talking about the wisdom of the ages?" I asked.

"Yes, I am," replied Andy.

Janet's eyes sparkled as she commented, "That's so interesting, Andy. I recently watched a debate on television among a well-known scholar, a philosopher, a scientist and a theologian. They were asked by the show's host if the wisdom of the ages was still of any value in this modern day. They appeared to have some difficulty coming to a definite conclusion. How would you answer that question, Andy?"

He thought for a short while and then replied, "The wisdom of the ages is a divine inner knowledge before the contamination of human thought. Such knowledge can never change, because it is spiritual by nature—not of this world, and has no form of its own. So my answer, in short, is:

"The wisdom of the ages is good for eternity."

Sensing that we had had enough, Andy rose and he and Emily left so that we could mull over what we had heard.

Later that evening after our supper, Janet and I talked about some of the gardener's unusual, yet simple, ideas—ideas that had already led us to some of the answers we have been seeking for a long time—powerful answers.

"It's a mystery to me," Janet told me, "that knowing so little about the workings of the principles can still have such a profound effect on someone's life. Imagine the tremendous suffering that could be alleviated throughout the world if there were practitioners with a degree in the *Three Principles*?"

"Yes," I replied. "It's a shame there aren't any right now, but Andy certainly seems hopeful there will be plenty in the future."

I wished her goodnight and left her shaking her head, saying the whole thing sounded too simple to be believed.

Chapter Ten

A Deeper Inquiry Into the Power of Thought

*I*t was another cloudless day and we were congratulating ourselves on our good fortune in having such great weather. I took full credit as I had bought an umbrella the first morning of our visit, and so, by the inexplicable laws of the weather gods, it was bound to stay sunny. At least, that's what I told Janet. She didn't seem entirely convinced but the blue skies held, so we were content. We were painfully aware that our time in England was running out and moments with Andy were to be taken whenever the opportunity arose.

This morning, he had agreed to meet us at a little shop that sold ice-cream cones topped by a flaky chocolate stick. Andy was happily munching when we arrived. Janet, who normally guarded her slim figure from such calorie-laden treats, put up a very weak protest when invited to indulge in their special French Vanilla. As far as I was concerned, two scoops of the incredibly rich peaches and cream was guiltless bliss.

As we finally wiped the last remnants of the cones from our faces with paper napkins, Andy asked us if he could put the shoe on the other foot for a change and ask us a simple question.

"Of course," I replied, now giving him my undivided attention.

"If you have the thought that you are insecure, how do you think you would feel?"

"I imagine I'd feel insecure," I answered.

"Now, that is simplicity in motion, is it not?" Andy asked.

Andy's statements always sounded too simplistic to have any validity and after this one I told him I didn't think life was that simple. Then I went on to explain to Andy that the reason we humans create insecure feelings is to warn us of danger and, without such feelings, we could get ourselves in a lot of trouble.

"Absolutely," Andy agreed. "I'm not judging whether you have or have not the right to create such feelings. I'm simply saying, it is immaterial *why* we create our feelings of insecurity or security. They all derive from our personal usage of this universal gift called *Thought*."

"I think that you and Janet are talking about what we do with our thoughts or what kind of behavior they lead to. What you have to realize is that I am talking about the *gift* of *Universal Thought,* before we do anything with it.

"Don't you see, Eric, this way we are discussing the very essence of *Universal Thought,* which is impersonal and totally neutral."

Whatever it was Janet was hearing had already affected her in the most positive way. I, too, had to acknowledge that Andy's help regarding my thoughts had a lot to do with my outlook on life. I told him how, in the couple of years since meeting him, my life had never been so good. I felt for the first time in my life that I was beginning to understand my profession. Then, sheepishly, I admitted to him that there had been times when I thought that he was way off base with his extraordinary philosophy, and that he had no idea what he was talking about.

"However," I said, "I remember one day I was sitting in my office, not thinking about anything in particular, when suddenly I saw to a deeper level that it was true that we all react to life according to our own thoughts. As you had said many times, Andy, my feelings are governed and manufactured from my own thinking.

"It was so simple and yet so profound, that I had to shake my head in disbelief. Here I was, a practicing psychologist, and I hadn't seen such an obvious fact before. It was a revelation to me— greater than anything I'd ever experienced before in my entire life.

"I'll tell you a little secret, Andy. When I was attending university, I used to dream of some day finding something that would bring me some contentment and happiness in my own life, something that I could pass on to my family and my clients. After I had that insight in my office, I thought to myself, 'Are my dreams coming true?' At that moment, I knew deep in my heart, I had to return to England and see you again."

Andy lowered his head for a moment. When he looked up his bright blue eyes were full of tears, he said he was honored that I would think that way of him. Then he asked me what my insight had been.

"Do you know, Andy, I don't think I could really explain what it was. It was a simple realization that my thoughts affected every part of my life. The experience itself was like a flash in time, but very powerful and meaningful to me, despite the fact that I failed to understand the deeper meaning of the experience itself."

Nodding his head Andy smiled at my story.

"On that same day I noticed that my clients and friends were doing exactly the same thing as I was. We were all creating our own interpretation of the reality we lived in, only we were doing it in different ways. It was then that I realized to a deeper level what you were trying to tell us about the power of *Thought*. That's when Janet and I decided to come and visit you again, to try to get a better understanding of your philosophical views regarding our psychological nature."

After a moment, Andy said, "The way I see it, Eric, the moment we were born we began using this magnificent gift of the *Three Principles* to guide us through life and to recognize our second home, called nature."

Andy's philosophy was captivating. I felt, however, that I needed a great deal more time to digest what he was saying.

"Could you clarify the connection between spirituality and psychology?" I asked him.

"You can't possibly find the secret to human behavior without walking on the spiritual side of life. Now please remember I am not talking religion, for the simple reason that religion has a form. What I'm telling you is the essence of all psychological experience here on earth. I'm talking in the impersonal, and right now we are talking about looking for some psychological answers. So I suggest we stick to a relevant subject, such as talking about the principles. Alright?"

Janet and I agreed that we would prefer to speak in terms of psychology.

"The other day, Eric, you asked me why I put so much importance on the *Three Principles*. I ask you to take a close look. When you do, you will see that it is through the innocently incorrect use of these three universal gifts that the lostness of humanity is born.

"You know, Eric, since the beginning of time, mankind has forged the tools to destroy himself within the armory of his own *thinking*. However, as human beings we also possess the same power within us to use our thoughts to build a heavenly mansion here on earth. This is why I say that the thoughts of mankind are the blueprints to all of humanity's future; just as they were in the past, so they always will be.

"Eric, what you have to realize is this: Deep in the celestial world of spirit lies the knowledge you long to find and this, my friend, has everything to do with your profession, because *Mind*, *Consciousness* and *Thought* are the very essence and seat of your profession."

After a long lull while Janet and I tried to assimilate Andy's latest assertion, Janet spoke quietly. "You know, Andy, many who come to me for advice often talk about unwanted thoughts coming into their heads. What would you say to someone regarding their unwanted thoughts. How can we stop negative, unwanted thoughts from entering our heads?"

Without hesitation, Andy replied, "You can't. They come too fast and if you try, you will soon find you are on a fool's mission. What you can do, however, is realize that your thoughts have no power of their own, only that which you give them. This is why constantly keeping your negative thoughts alive is unhealthy. My advice is keep away from people who, innocently, take you back into the past and help you to fill your head with negative thoughts and sadness.

"Such practices strip away all hope of recovery and will keep you in the dark for the rest of your life. Never forget that hope is a very important ally that often leads to miraculous things."

Completely gripped by what she was hearing, Janet murmured, "So what I hear you say is that everyone on earth has what is called a free will, and with this free will we have the power to pick the thoughts that we want to become alive, and ignore and discard the ones we don't. We don't have to act on every thought!"

"That is it precisely," Andy replied, "for example, we are exercising it now by having this discussion."

I was about to dispute his point of view, when all at once I saw that his words were true. I was picking which of my thoughts I wanted to use in our ongoing dialogue. As I was thinking that, I heard Andy's voice saying, "Never forget, Eric, we live in a world governed by our thoughts and negative thoughts can enter our heads so fast that it is virtually impossible to control them. However, if you can see that they are only thoughts and you refuse to put life into them, they are harmless. If you can do this, you may be surprised by the positive effect it can have on your life."

I was about to ask Andy another question when he suddenly lifted his hands in the air, shook his head and said, "Please, no more questions. Stop asking question after question. Give yourself a little peace to absorb what we have been talking about."

Then he suggested to Janet and I,

"Have some faith in yourselves
and know that somewhere deep inside,
Beyond your ego, beyond the personal self,
lies a beautiful flower waiting to unfold,
And it is the light of true knowledge
that will make it blossom."

With these words, he walked away leaving us with many things to reflect upon.

Chapter Eleven
Simplicity

*O*ur next meeting with Andy found the three of us relaxing by a riverbank and watching a couple in a small boat as they rowed by. Occasionally one of us would comment on the beauty of the scene, but mostly we just sat quietly, in a contemplative state, enjoying the day. Eventually we began another conversation in which I told Andy that there was so much in life I had yet to learn that it felt like I was a student all over again.

"Eric, we are all students of life, seeking answers to many things, and we always will be as long as we have the breath of life in us. I am happy to know that you are not like so many people who think that once they have graduated from university, they are at the end of their search for knowledge. The search for such knowledge is endless as time itself. The beauty is, each time you find a piece of this mystical puzzle it brings you more answers. It assists you to see beyond the word, to the true meaning. It is with your realization of this true meaning that the metaphors of the wise become a living reality.

"Will you two do me a favor?" Andy asked.

"Of course," we replied, "anything. What is it?"

"The next time you go down into a low mood, don't try to analyze why. If you do you will drive yourself crazy as you find a thousand reasons you can adopt to explain the why. Analyzing yourself is like a dog chasing its own tail; it's the perfect weapon for the delusionary ego to manipulate your belief in the phantoms inside your head.

"I would like to bet you five pounds to a penny, that when you began your profession as therapists and were first introduced to analyzing, it almost drove you and all your friends crazy."

Janet hung her head momentarily, and then with a huge smile remarked how embarrassing it was to even think about what she had put her parents through. "How they put up with me, I'll never know. I analyzed them night and day. My poor father thought at one time that I was becoming a little touched in the head and he strongly advised me to choose another profession. I hate to admit this but all the time I was studying, I'd go to bed and my brain would start analyzing all sorts of different situations until I was so confused, I felt like screaming. I seriously thought about taking my father's advice."

I couldn't help but smile, as I admitted, "My story was much the same as Janet's. The only difference was that it was my older brother and a few close friends who were the guinea pigs."

Janet feigned a look of shock. "Eric, I'm surprised at such behavior from you."

"Andy," I asked, "what do you do when you go into a lower mood, if you don't analyze—how do you discover the cause—unless of course the cause is blatantly obvious?"

"If it isn't obvious to me why I'm in a low mood, then I look for simplicity," Andy replied.

His answer didn't make any sense to me and I asked him to clarify what he meant when he said he would look for simplicity. It seemed to me that if he were looking for simplicity he would only discover causes that were blatantly obvious.

My question brought a gleam to Andy's eyes. "I told you not too long ago that the answer lies in simplicity, and it's all connected to the quality of your thoughts. As simple as it sounds, I would look and see that the quality of my thoughts had dropped to a lower state, creating a mood change. Upon realizing this lowered state, I would be open to allowing my mental state to rise again, automatically. I can guarantee you, Eric, if you do as I suggest, you will be rewarded beyond your wildest dreams."

Janet asked Andy if he could explain to her just one more time about the *Power of Thought*.

Andy sighed deeply as if to say "Here we go again," then began another explanation. "The *Power of Thought* is spiritual in nature and is an element that can never be broken down into components. On the other hand, personal thoughts can be broken down endlessly. A very important point to consider is how we use such a magnificent gift to guide us through life. Now again I ask you to note that I am not judging anyone, I am simply saying: Use your free will and the *Three Principles* wisely.

"Use them with integrity and harm no other human being. If you do these things, then you will be guided through life on an even keel. To put it simply:

"Universal Consciousness is purity of consciousness,
Universal Mind is purity of Mind,
Universal Thought is purity of Thought.

"And based on these three statements we can see why the wise have always told us that love is the answer."

The gardener's statement that love is connected to *Universal Mind, Consciousness and Thought* shocked me and I told him so.

"Why should that surprise you?" he asked.

"Andy, please don't get me wrong. I'm captivated by some of the things you're saying, but I'm afraid I fail to see the connection between love, *Mind, Consciousness and Thought.*"

Andy smiled at my remark and then answered. "Let's put it this way. The purer your *Mind* is, the more loving, caring and understanding a person you will be. Right?

"The purer your *consciousness,* the more understanding and loving a person you will be.

"The purer your *thoughts,* the more thoughtful and loving a person you will be."

"Andy," Janet asked, "please be patient with me, but we're going back home soon, and I'd like to get this as straight in my mind as I can. Would you please, one more time, differentiate between personal consciousness and *Universal Consciousness?*"

Breaking into another of his knowing smiles, the gardener replied, "Now, that's a tricky question to answer. Let me try to express it this way.

"*Universal Consciousness* is a gift that we are all blessed with at birth; it allows us to realize the existence of creation and to be consciously aware of the reality we live in. It's very important to remember, Janet, that every day of our lives we use this gift called *Consciousness* to understand and observe life.

"*Universal Consciousness* is the divine understanding of all things and does not belong to you or me. However, our personal selves have the honor and privilege to use this gift to guide us through life.

"Now then, what you are calling your personal consciousness is the sum total of whatever you and your own private thought system are aware of, or ever will be aware of in this lifetime.

"And one thing well worth taking note of is that our personal consciousness can change from moment to moment and, at times, can become quite unstable.

"On the other hand, *Universal Consciousness* can never change, because it has no form. It just is. This gift of *Consciousness* allows us to understand both the world of form and the formless world that lies within. I can guarantee you:

"You can have Consciousness without understanding, but you can't have understanding without Consciousness!

"From the tiniest atom to the greatest mountain on earth, all life is one infinite ball of pulsating consciousness. When you can understand such a fact, you will see that it is in *Universal Consciousness* that we find the secret to the oneness of life and the secret to all quantum theory, and where everything in this world is all interconnected."

Andy's words took me by surprise. I asked him where he studied quantum physics and his answer surprised me even more. "I have never studied quantum physics in my life. As a matter of fact I have little or no idea what quantum physics entails. I only know that the *Three Principles* of *Universal Mind, Consciousness and Thought* hold the secret to the oneness of this exterior world and the formless spiritual world. These are the unifying principles that Dr. Einstein was searching for."

I looked over at Janet and by the look on her face it was apparent that she was just as surprised by Andy's reply as I was. I asked myself, how can this be? Surely an ordinary gardener can't possibly have the answer that such brilliant physicists couldn't find? "Andy, surely you don't expect me to believe what you are saying?"

With a shrug of his shoulders Andy replied, "Not really Eric. After all, what I'm trying to tell you is the greatest mystical secret on earth. What you have to understand is that there is a dimension to life beyond this reality you now know, a dimension beyond this world of time, space and matter. This world that I am talking about is a world of formless spiritual energy that lies beyond all the logic and mathematics that you and I are used to. Remember, I once told you that this physical reality we live in derives from a formless spiritual energy brought into being by our usage of the three universal principles."

Andy knew he had shocked us with such statements and with a smile on his face he remarked, "Didn't I once tell you that the *Three Principles* hold the secret not just to psychology and psychiatry but to life?"

Neither Janet nor I said a word. We just sat flabbergasted, not knowing how to reply to the gardener's words.

Finally Andy said, "Everyone on earth has this spiritual secret deep within their consciousness and if you ever wake up to this fact, your life will never be the same again. This secret is where the external physical world and the formless spiritual world become *one*—sometimes known as the great oneness—where everything is interconnected.

"Quantum physics?" Janet questioned uncertainly.

"Exactly," replied Andy, "and even more important to you, Janet, the answers to *all* human experience and behavior here on earth."

"So what I hear you say is: The secret to the *Three Principles* not only holds the answer to psychology, but also some answers to physics?"

"Correct, Janet, and much, much more."

Janet raised her forefinger in the air as if she had just remembered something. "Do you know,

Andy, about a month ago I was watching a television show and there were three physicists talking way beyond my understanding, then two of them surprised me when they said what they were looking for was something called *God Mind*. When they said that I thought about you and wondered what you would think about their statement."

"Janet, what do you think I have been talking about all this time? *God Mind* and *Universal Mind* are one and the same thing."

Janet slowly shook her head remarking, "I don't understand what you just said and you have definitely boggled my mind."

Andy and Emily burst into laughter at Janet's last statement and the bewildered look on our faces.

Janet asked Emily if she understood what Andy was talking about. Emily, smiling from ear to ear at our perplexity, remarked, "Don't ask me what the man means, I'm still as surprised and confused as you are at some things Andy says. This is why I believe that we should all learn to respect each other's way of searching for such knowledge and not get caught up in the trap of thinking, 'My way is better than yours, and my way is the only way.' One thing I have learned throughout the years is to keep an open mind and a respect for other people's religious, political and personal beliefs—it may surprise you what you may learn. I've known Andy now for many years and every time I think I know what he is talking about he pulls a surprise on me, just as he did today."

Then Andy suggested that Janet and I should turn our focus on the psyche. "I would suggest you look at the true nature of *Mind* and its relationship to all human functioning because it contains the secret to all psychological experience here on earth and is the seat of all consciousness."

"I love what you're saying, Andy, but you make it sound unbelievably simple, and to me, it's anything but simple," Janet lamented.

The gardener smiled, heaved an enormous, dramatic sigh, and then repeated the words, "Simplicity, simplicity, simplicity. Why is simplicity so complicated?"

Janet and I looked at each other, smiling at the gardener's answer. Janet put the question I had just been thinking to myself. "Andy, I don't understand what you mean. Why do you believe the answer is simple?"

"Because you already know the answer, but somewhere along the line you have forgotten!" he answered. "And I can tell you:

"In the quiet chambers of your mind
Lies the knowledge you seek.

Not in a complicated search,
But only from a positive mind can you ever find
the answer to this mystical puzzle."

"Why do you say that only from a positive mind can such knowledge be found?"

"Because, Janet, such knowledge is created from a wisdom that is held in trust for eternity and only when our minds are in a quiet, positive state can such knowledge be turned into a reality.

"This is why so many people throughout the world take the time to meditate. It quiets their minds and allows this inner knowledge to create a living reality."

Janet explained that her friend Peter used to meditate a lot but he still suffered from an overactive mind.

"Perhaps he depended on the *technique* of meditating too much," Andy answered. "Many people I know suffer with the same delusionary belief that if they sit and meditate for 'x' number of hours per day, they will gain the knowledge they seek. Believe me, Janet, that is definitely not so. I know many people who fall into this trap and I haven't as yet seen one of them find what they were looking for."

Then he started to laugh and told us that just recently he met someone who told him that he meditated four hours every day and how wonderful he felt after he finished. "He said sitting so long was very painful, but bearing the pain he went through was well worth it. I asked him how he could possibly find peace of mind when he was in pain but he never answered me. He just went on to tell me that his teacher could sit for seven hours in pain and that soon both he and his teacher were heading to China where they were going to take lessons from someone who could sit for ten hours.

"I tried to tell him to beware of getting the state of meditation and the act of meditating mixed up, otherwise his quest for a peaceful mind would all be in vain. However, my words fell on deaf ears. He asked me how I would seek a peaceful mind and I suggested that he should take a good look and try to understand how the *Three Principles* held the secret to a peaceful mind, but again my words fell on deaf ears. As far as I know he is now in China sitting in pain—looking for a peaceful mind."

Janet remarked, "I have many clients who meditate on a regular basis, yet they still have deep mental problems. I often wondered why this is."

"Do you know, Janet, many people don't realize there are many levels of meditation?"

With a surprised look on her face, Janet remarked that she never thought there could be different levels of meditation, "I always thought you were in the state of meditation or you weren't."

"I'm with you Janet—I've never heard anyone describe meditation that way. Andy, would you care to elaborate on such a statement?"

"The way I see it, Eric, the state of meditation you are in and the state of consciousness you are in are the same thing, only the words differ to describe the level of thought you are functioning from. However, if you can find out how the *Three Principles* work, then you can naturally function throughout your life in what some people call a state of meditation without going though the technique of meditating."

Andy's explanation of meditation and levels of consciousness being the same really surprised me and again I could see there was more to the *Three Principles* than Janet and I were aware of. Again, I felt it was necessary to ask Andy if he could explain what he was trying to tell us in a different way.

He answered my question with one of his own. "Why do you think some of your patients are being cured from their mental imbalances and what has happened to both of you that took you to an understanding beyond anything that you were taught in school?"

"I guess it's because we started to understand the workings of the *Three Principles* and now we can supply a better explanation to our clients of how mind and consciousness work in daily life," I answered.

"Exactly," Andy replied. "Don't you see that it is because your consciousness has risen to a higher level of understanding that both of you have had such success with your clients? From this new level of understanding, you and your clients have had insights that have allowed you to drop volumes of unnecessary and harmful thought, thereby leaving you with a clearer, more peaceful state of mind.

"Haven't you told me over and over again how peaceful your minds have become and how all the stress you were having from talking with patients has vanished without sitting and meditating? May I suggest that you have found what you were looking for by acknowledging the power of the *Three Principles*? Let me also suggest to you that you have gone into a more permanent and higher state of meditation."

"Wow, I never thought about it that way," Janet remarked. "So what I hear you say is, we are putting our clients into a higher state of meditation or consciousness by explaining to them how the *Three Principles* work instead of them having to go through the ritual of meditating. Could this be why all the great mystics throughout time have told us to beware of rituals and dogma as they will lead you away from the truth?"

"That's exactly what you have been doing. By avoiding the traps of rituals and dogma, your results have shot beyond anything now known in the field. Once your profession sees this for a fact, the old theories you have been taught will completely vanish from the face of this earth. Then there will be healings beyond your wildest imagination."

Janet looked stunned by Andy's words and I was bowled over, once again made speechless by what I was hearing. After the longest time, I asked Andy to explain in another way why this knowledge was not well known throughout the world.

"Eric, haven't I told you before, the principles we are talking about have always existed, yet they are one of the greatest secrets on earth. I doubt very much if many people since the beginning of time have known about them." Andy smiled at the confused look on my face, rolled back his eyes, shook his head and let out a deep sigh. Then he smiled patiently and said, "Before time, space and matter, we were without form. When we were born into this physical world, our five senses were activated by our use of the three spiritual gifts called *Mind, Consciousness and Thought.*

"The very moment we enter this world of form, we are immediately misguided by the vision of this

Great Spiritual Illusion called creation. It is with this vision of creation that the delusionary ego is born and where we lose our purity of thought and our true identity."

"What exactly do you mean when you say we lose our true identity and the purity of thought at birth?" Janet asked.

"This is the way I see it, Janet. At birth, we are innocent babes born into a foreign land, and our eyes see only this divine illusion that we live in.

"That's why I say to both of you, to find the secret to all human thinking and behavior you will have to reverse the way you think, and instead of concentrating so much on behavior, as Dr. Freud and many others innocently suggested, look for the innate knowledge that we are all blessed with.

"This innate knowledge, sometimes known as wisdom, will not only cure the behavior, but it will also prevent most problems from occurring in the first place."

"I can see that," Janet replied. "Gosh, the very thought of there being such an answer gives me goose bumps."

"Never forget, Luv, I am talking in the *Impersonal*."

"Andy, I can see that you are talking in complete neutrality and I respect you for that. However,

I want to know how we access this knowledge that you keep talking about?"

"Remember, I told you that the knowledge you seek is beyond the word, and beyond our five senses? And, if you look closely at all the words of the wise, you will see that regardless of how they expressed themselves, they all pointed to the fact that what you seek lies within. Another way to say that is, what you seek is innate.

"I am suggesting to you, to find such knowledge you should stop looking and just be,

"For it is in the silent chambers of your mind
Such knowledge is incubated and brought to life.

"Try to be content with what you have, and it may surprise you how the quality of your life could change for the better. Never forget, contentment is a state of being that always comes clothed in a positive feeling. Contentment brings peace of mind and happiness into one's life."

Many of the gardener's theories and ideas were things I had secretly wondered about since I was a little boy, but was always too afraid to ask anyone about. I felt that Andy's teachings were, to say the least, profound, though totally different from what I was taught or was used to.

I was certainly never taught, nor had I ever thought, that mental health lay inside everyone. Listening to Andy, I suddenly realized what he meant when he said that wisdom was purity of thought. What he was suggesting was that we go back into our subconscious and retrieve our innate wisdom, before it became tainted by our own flawed thoughts and ideas. I asked him how this could possibly be done and he answered, "Again I tell you:

"By using the three magical principles of Mind, Consciousness and Thought as purely as you can."

From my previous experiences of listening to Andy talk I knew that he had a habit of leaving you with a cliffhanger and today he did just that, announcing to Janet and me that he had to go home to meet some people who were coming to his house. Smiling, he said, "But I'll be back in a couple of hours in case you have any more questions."

When he left, Janet and I once again tried to figure out his unusual philosophy. After intellectually straining our brains for half an hour we finally gave up and burst into peals of laughter at the futility of our endeavoring to understand what we had heard—or indeed, what he had said. To try to quell our racing minds we strolled through the village, sightseeing and shopping. Unexpectedly, my mind was so calm it was as if I were tranquilized, yet everything looked clear-edged and bright and all the vendors seemed particularly friendly.

"It's so wonderful to be in England again," Janet commented. "I'm sure I've never felt so good in all my life."

"Me, too, Janet, I feel like I'm walking on cloud nine and I don't really know why. I just have this feeling that we are about to find something incredible."

"I have that same feeling, Eric. That talk we had last night regarding Andy's belief that we have freedom of thought and a free will, for some reason it really got me and today I'm still trying to figure it all out."

We agreed to ask him on his return to explain the difference between the two.

Chapter Twelve
Freedom of Choice and Evolution

*T*wo hours later, we met Andy at his favorite café and we continued our conversation as planned. Janet explained to Andy that, as always after a talk with him, we were a little confused. "We were wondering what the difference is between our free will and our freedom of thought?"

He replied with no hesitation, "They are both the same power with two different names."

Observing the mystified look on our faces, he said, "Just think about it for a while and I'm sure that you'll see that one cannot possibly have a free will, without the freedom of thought. As I just said, they are both the same power in a different disguise."

Janet sat in deep contemplation for several minutes and then explained to Andy that there are many scholars who would disagree that there even is such a thing as a free will.

Smiling, Andy asked Janet, " If their personal opinion regarding life isn't their free will in action, what is it?

"Now remember, Janet, there is a vast difference between your free will and your freedom of action. Nobody can take away your free will. Your free will is whatever you think is right or wrong. It allows you to see life through your own eyes.

"But freedom of action is not always possible for any number of reasons. For example, we could have anarchy if everybody just did what they wanted. This is why we need laws to protect the community as a whole."

After a short silence Janet responded, "I never thought of it that way."

"Now bear in mind," Andy continued, "I'm not judging who is right or who is wrong, nor am I saying one belief is better than another. I'm simply saying that the same process creates all our personal beliefs. Anything that you are aware of must come through your personal thought system by using the *Three Principles* and your free will.

"Think of it this way, Janet. We are all thinking creatures. Inside our heads we judge what we believe and what we disbelieve. This is our free will in action and every moment of our lives we make decisions using our own thinking. This is why we human beings were blessed with this glorious gift of *Thought*.

"Please understand, I am simply trying to tell you that there's a deeper level of understanding of your profession than either of you are aware of at the present moment. That's why it gives me so much pleasure to hear that your last visit to England was so beneficial to you."

Janet shrugged her shoulders, glanced over at me with a look of wonderment, and then nodded her head in acknowledgement of Andy's words. "I can't begin to understand everything you were saying, Andy, but I would certainly like to thank you for all your help. You've made a tremendous contribution to my quality of life."

Andy shyly answered, "You know, Janet, at times like this I feel a little embarrassed at the thought of my suggesting something to you regarding your own profession. After all, I'm only an old, retired gardener."

Janet reached out and took Andy's hand in hers. "Andy, I am absolutely enthralled by your beliefs regarding the workings of the mind. It's like a breath of fresh air to both Eric and me."

"I appreciate your kind words, Luv, but all I'm telling you is simple common sense. As far as I'm concerned, for any profession to grow, regardless of which profession it may be, there has to be a shift into a higher state of understanding.

"I realize that for some people to accept new findings it can require courage, for they may start to believe that their training was all in vain—of course that's nonsense.

"It's simply a matter of evolution and evolution has been happening everyday since day one and it will continue to do so."

"That's exactly how I felt," Janet remarked. "I thought to myself, 'Have I gone through all this training for nothing?' Then one night it came to me—if I listened to what Andy was saying, surely I would have the common sense and the ability to see for myself what works and what doesn't. After all, I still had my old training, only now I have a little extra. Maybe!"

I laughed at Janet's way of putting things.

"The medical doctors do this all the time and once they find something that works better, they cast away the old and work with the new," she commented.

I explained to Andy, "When Einstein came up with his famous equation $E=mc^2$, it was not arrived at directly through his formal training. That's one of the reasons the scientific community had so much trouble accepting his theory. When it was finally accepted, as you just said, Janet, they cast away their old ideas and looked at the new. There's no shame cast upon the old ways—it's a matter of evolution—the discovery of something new and better."

Janet looked over at me and shrugged her shoulders, "I wonder if anything like that will ever happen in our field?"

"Certainly, Luv, and if you look carefully, you will see that both of you have already jumped the boundaries of time and gone ahead of whatever you used to think regarding the workings of your own profession."

Andy's confidence was astounding. We were flabbergasted by the assurance in his voice and the certainty with which he stated his conviction that we had advanced well beyond our formal training. I asked him how he could be so sure that we had.

"That I can't explain to you, Eric, and to be truthful, I have no intention of even trying. You must see it for yourself, and when you do, I guarantee that you will find difficulty believing the simplicity of your find."

Both Janet and I just sat there, sipping our coffee and wondering what the old gardener was talking about.

Then very casually he said, "Let's put it this way. Haven't both of you been telling me of the positive changes in your lives and your work?"

"Yes, we have," I replied.

"Now I ask you, was it your training that brought your new-found success, or was it something that you discovered deep within the recesses of your *own* consciousness?"

"I never looked at it that way," Janet remarked, "but it is true—I know understanding even the smallest amount about the workings of the principles and how they relate to our daily life brings incredible benefits."

I completely agreed with Janet. "It's becoming more and more apparent to me that the little knowledge we've found regarding the workings of our thoughts is responsible for creating our successes. Andy, I feel there is so much more to learn—at times I worry I'm not doing enough to help my clients."

Andy shook his head, saying, "If I were you, Eric, I wouldn't sell myself too short. If you pair look at the results you've had in the past year, you will see that both of you are doing a lot more good for your clients than you realize.

"You know, Eric, once upon a time an old friend told me,

"You can tell how many seeds there are in an apple,
But you can't tell how many apples there are in a seed.

"So, I'm telling you both, never underestimate the help in the seeds of hope that you are bringing to your clients."

We thanked Andy for his encouraging words, and soon after we said goodbye for the day and headed back to the hotel for a late afternoon nap.

Chapter Thirteen
The Oneness of Life

*E*mily had strongly encouraged us to see the old village of Cockington, saying that it was reputed to be one of England's most picturesque, so we decided to spend our last full day there, and invited Emily and Andy to join us on our visit to see the sights. They eagerly accepted our invitation and we made arrangements to meet at the blacksmith's shop at eleven o'clock.

We arrived early at the small parking lot, found a shady space for the car and followed the signs toward a group of stone cottages. We were pleasantly surprised to see horse-drawn carriages ready to take visitors around the manicured grounds, but we chose to walk through the village toward the blacksmith's shop. We were entranced by the fact that every house and shop had a thatched roof, which, we later discovered, each bore the proud signature of the tradesman who had done the job. A design cut along the roof-ridge or a bird modeled from thatch at the corner identified the thatcher.

A feeling of timelessness overtook us, creating an illusion of walking through an 18th-century novel. We revelled in the beauty of the village and grounds of the manor house that had existed for 500 years and more. The grand old house, with its parks and gardens, was imbued with a sense of privilege. With time suddenly in slow motion, we felt no need to hurry, even though we eagerly anticipated our meeting with Andy and Emily, especially knowing this would be the last time we'd see them before we had to fly back to the States.

We had no difficulty locating the old blacksmith's shop where they were already waiting for us. There was an unbelievable feeling about the place that no words could express, a feeling of age and tranquility and the wonder of countless lives, each with its own joys and sorrows, lived out in this beautiful setting. I looked over at Janet and she was absolutely beaming. Suddenly I was overwhelmed by an intense longing, wishing Norma could be here to share this experience.

Then I heard Janet exclaim excitedly, "Look, there's a set of medieval stocks!" She immediately insisted on having her picture taken in them. Emily assisted her to get into the instrument of punishment. Once she was seated with hands and feet and head held firmly in place by the heavy wooden stocks, laughing uproariously, Janet had us take several pictures of her. Then both Janet and Emily insisted it was my turn to be held prisoner in the stocks, so reluctantly I gave in and Janet snapped several incriminating photos.

Nearby, we discovered a delightful little open-air restaurant where we decided to have lunch. From the seating area a lush lawn ran down toward a fish pond set amidst tall rushes and a ring of bright flowers. Within an open-sided gazebo that stood between us and the pond a quartet of smiling teenage girls played baroque music. Listening to them, I felt that I was in the middle of some mystical dream; never had I felt so tranquil or at peace. I just wanted to enjoy the good space I was in. As we lingered over our meal, the quartet finished their performance and was heartily applauded by an appreciative audience that had gathered in and around the restaurant.

After completing our lunch with "a good strong cuppa tea" and a rich trifle dessert, we decided to continue our exploration of the village and wandered on. The afternoon sun glowed on the old ivy-covered stone cottages, while the sound of water splashing through the wooden water wheel provided a soothing background to the peaceful setting. An enormous variety of trees, everything from ancient oaks and beeches to graceful willows, dotted the grounds, huge rhododendrons lined one side of the winding drive, and many imported specimen trees stood in solitary splendor in the park, carefully positioned by generations of owners so that their beauty and rarity could readily impress visiting gentry. The former manor house, now devoted to craft demonstrations, had a huge, walled rose garden containing a fragrant collection of old and new varieties. Nearby, mossy gravestones around the stone church bore witness to past residents of the village, at rest under more rhododendron bushes and sweet-smelling lilacs. I wondered what stories they had to tell and what sights had been seen over the centuries in this quiet corner of England. We had stopped to rest on a bench, when the clip clop of horses' hooves caught our attention. Two gleaming chestnut horses were being led back to the stables, where they would be groomed and given a well-earned rest until their next tour of duty.

Janet remarked, "This has to be one of the most heavenly places I've ever seen. It's just occurred to me," she confided, "that this would be a perfect place to have my honeymoon."

We sat quietly, just absorbing the splendor of our surroundings. I thought to myself, "For all the times you may see England on television, it can't possibly prepare you for the real McCoy." The age of many of the buildings fascinated me. Seeing houses that were built before the *Mayflower* left for America gave me goose bumps.

Emily and Andy and I settled on the park bench while Janet spread her sweater to sit on the newly mowed lawn. For quite some time Janet and I mused aloud about what had happened in our lives to make them seem so new and wonderful. We watched the horses and carts filled with holiday makers go by, then for some inexplicable reason, I asked Andy a question that I'm sure has been asked since the beginning of time.

"What do you think life is?"

To my surprise, he answered, "Life is whatever you think it is."

"That may be so, Andy, but what do you, personally, think it is?"

Andy thought for a moment, then replied. "I would say,

"Life as we know it is one gigantic ball of energy,
Whether in form or formless."

"Is that your answer?" I asked, amazed by Andy's short, simplistic answer.

"That's it," he replied.

"Would you elucidate for me, Andy. Why do you describe life the way you do?"

"Do you remember, Eric, I once told you that this physical world stems from a formless energy that exists before time, space and matter?"

"Yes I do, but I didn't quite understand that, and I would love to hear you explain what you meant, once more."

Andy looked at me, at Janet, then back at me, apparently considering his response. Janet and I eagerly awaited his reply. Then he finally said,

"When the formless energy of which I speak joins this physical reality, we call it matter. However, regardless of the form it has taken in this life, it is still the same formless spiritual energy—but in countless disguises."

Confused by Andy's reply, Janet just sat and looked puzzled for some minutes. Then sheepishly she admitted, "I still don't get the concept of a form-less energy. Do you mean formless like electricity?"

"No, not at all, Janet. Electricity is of this world and has a form. The formless energy I speak of is not of this world."

"I think your theory of formless energy is very interesting," Janet said, "but such a theory is quite abstract and could never be proven. After all, how can anyone prove that such a thing as formless energy exits?"

The old gardener smiled and agreed with Janet that it would be impossible to prove the existence of such energy. "So in answer to your question," he replied, "it can't."

"What makes you believe that such formless energy exists?" I asked.

"That, Eric, I can't explain, but I can assure you, it does exist. Never forget:

"Just because a blind man can't see the heavens,
Doesn't mean the stars don't exist."

As I listened, I started to relate what Andy was saying to some philosophical and spiritual books I had read. I asked him if he was talking about "The Great Nothingness" that some of the eastern mystics have talked about.

"I guess you could call the formlessness I speak of 'The Great Nothingness.' Yes, that would definitely fit what I am trying to convey to you."

"I find such ideas as 'formlessness' and 'The Great Nothingness' pretty intriguing. Just what are you calling 'formlessness'?" Janet asked.

"It's like this, Luv: The formless energy I speak of is a spiritual energy before the creation of this physical world. Once this formless energy joins this world of form, we call it creation, or the physical reality that we live in. The transformation of this formless energy into this physical world is what some of the great mystics throughout time have called 'The Great Illusion.' That is why I can assure you that this physical world we live in is all connected to time, space and matter—which all have illusionary values."

Once again Andy's words left me wondering and by the expression on her face I could see that Janet was equally perplexed.

"Andy, I have absolutely no idea what you are talking about," she sighed. "What in heaven's name do you mean by time, space and matter all having illusionary values?"

The old gardener smiled broadly at the bewildered look on our faces, then pointing to a nearby tree he said, "Do you see that tree over there?"

"Yes," Janet answered.

"Well, what do you think is between you and that tree?"

"Nothing," Janet answered.

"Wrong!" Andy replied, "There are particles of air, dust, water and many other unseen forms between you and that tree."

Both Emily and Andy were grinning from ear to ear at the look of mystification on Janet's face. Then the old gardener said, "Think of it this way, Janet, what I am saying is this: Literally everything in this physical world is created from the same formless energy.

"Now I want you to look carefully and you will see that if this is so, then you are also a product of this formless energy.

"Then if you look a little closer you will see that all the particles of dust, air, water and a host of other little things present are all created from this same formless energy, but expressed in an endless variety of forms.

"Last, but not least, we have the tree, which is also created from the same formless energy, but in the form of a tree. Therefore, common sense tells me, the division between you and the tree must be an illusion—if everything in this universe is created from the same energy.

"When this is seen, everything is One; just as you and I are particles of the whole."

His explanation struck me like a bolt of lightning. "Are you talking about the Oneness of life?" I inquired.

"Yes, that's exactly what I'm talking about," Andy replied.

"You know, Andy, in many books I've read and in my searching throughout the Far East I've often heard masters talk about the Oneness of life, but I've never heard it explained in such a simple way. Come to think of it, I never did hear anyone try to explain such a mystical phenomenon. Can you elaborate a little more on the Oneness of life?"

Andy stared at the ground in deep thought for a while before answering, "This Oneness I speak of has been explained in many ways. For instance, some say there can only be One God and this is true because,

"God is the energy of all things,
Whether in form or formless.

"This is 'The Great Oneness' of life that the sagacious have spoken about since the beginning of time.

"I am sure in all the reading and traveling you have done you have heard the saying, 'I am that which I seek,' meaning, 'I am the same energy that I seek—we are One'."

"Andy, I am definitely familiar with that saying, but for some reason I prefer what you are saying. Your ideas and concepts absolutely fascinate me. Do you realize you are talking about physics?"

Andy smiled and looked a little embarrassed. He dropped his head and said, "To be truthful with you, Eric, I never thought about it that way, because I know nothing about physics. I only know what I know.

"But this I can tell you, once you start talking about the world of formlessness the laws of physics start to break down and are no longer applicable. This is why I think we should talk about the form."

"How can you say with such assurance that the laws of physics break down when you talk about formlessness, especially when you say you know nothing about physics?" I demanded.

The old gardener gazed intently into my eyes as though looking for the slightest glimmer of understanding. For the first time, I could hear a tone of frustration beginning to creep into his voice as he said, "Haven't I told you again and again that the *Three Principles* of *Mind, Consciousness* and *Thought* cover all sciences, all psychological beliefs, all philosophies, all religions and all human behavior?"

It was difficult for me to believe what Andy was saying. All the time I'd known Andy I had never related what he was saying about the principles to physics. Up until this point, I thought that he was only trying to link them to psychology and with a sudden sense of shame I realized why Andy had once said to us that the *Three Principles* weren't only for the chosen few, meaning the field of psychology, but for everyone.

Janet shook her head slowly and murmured, "You're blowing my mind again, Andy. I'm just now starting to see that the applications are never ending."

Andy smiled at Janet's remark. "This I can tell you, Luv. If you ever have the good fortune to discover the true nature of the *Three Principles*, that's when your search for the knowledge of the very essence of your profession will bear fruit.

"That is when you will understand the correlation between *Mind* and *Soul*, or, being psychologists, you could say finding the correlation between *Mind* and *Psyche*.

"That is when you will find your answers to human behavior.

"That is when you will help people, taking them from darkness into the light of mental health— if they have the ears to listen and the eyes to see."

Then, very respectfully, Janet asked Andy how he could be so sure of such statements.

"I'm afraid, Luv, that is impossible for me explain to you. However, this I can tell you: As you start to realize the true nature of *Mind*, you will start to unravel the psychological puzzle you have been looking at and discover the answers you seek."

"What is the true nature of the spiritual *Mind*?" I asked.

Andy searched my eyes with his, once again seeking a spark of comprehension, as he replied, "There are many names you can call it. *The Spiritual Mind*, *Divine Mind*, or if you prefer, *Universal Mind* is God. Again I tell you:

> *"God is the energy of all things,*
> *whether in form or formless.*

"This is why only God can be infinite."

Andy knew he had me baffled and chortled to himself at the look on my face as I asked him, "What has infinity got to do with all of this?"

"If you had been listening more openly and less intently you would have heard me explain that to you already!

"Eric, you are trying too hard to figure out my words intellectually, instead of listening beyond my words and finding a deeper dimension of thought. May I suggest to you that we move back into physics and put it this way: Some people have the misconception that infinity has something to do with endless time, space or matter. Believe me, this is not so. Infinity has nothing to do with time, space or matter. Infinity is not a quantity.

> *"Infinity is the energy of all things,*
> *whether in form or formless."*

Janet and I sat with our mouths open, staring at Andy, once again having no response for such an incredible statement. Then he expanded on his theory, "One could say,

> *"All matter is created from a formless energy that has*
> *no body of its own, until it comes into this world*
> *of time, space and matter."*

I described to Andy how some beliefs in the Far East and India talk about looking for the True Self. "They say if you ever do find your True Self, then you will be enlightened. Is this what you are talking about?"

"Yes," Andy replied, "that is exactly what I'm talking about. When the True Self is realized, then the great awakening takes place within the consciousness of a human being."

When I looked over at Janet she was weeping quietly, then Andy gathered her into his arms and held her, soothing her, telling her he knew she was a beautiful human being. "Some day, God willing, you will find the answer to the riddle of how all of the *Three Principles* are One."

We sat as though spellbound, each enthralled in our own thoughts, our own understanding of Andy's words, allowing the silence to lengthen like the shadows that were beginning to appear under some of the larger trees. Finally Emily spoke, gently breaking the enchantment.

"I'm sorry but Andy and I will have to leave soon. We're expecting guests and have to be back home before six o'clock. It's been so lovely seeing you both again."

I couldn't believe the time had gone by so fast and it was now almost time to leave Torquay. Eyes brimming, Janet embraced Emily and thanked her and Andy for all their hospitality and kindness. Emily replied, "It's been our pleasure. I hope you can arrange to return to Torquay on your honeymoon, and if you do Andy and I would love to meet your husband."

With perfect timing, just as we were saying our goodbyes, a horse and buggy arrived to carry Emily and Andy back to their car. I shook Andy's hand. "Thank you, Andy. I think this last week has been the most interesting and probably the most important of my life." Then I embraced Emily and thanked her for all her love and caring. Janet's eyes had now overflowed and, tears streaming down her face, she threw her arms around Andy's neck, kissed his cheek and thanked him for all his hospitality and wise words. Then for a second time Janet threw her arms around Emily and held her for the longest time whispering the words, "Thank you, thank you."

Janet stepped back, wiping her eyes. Andy helped Emily into the carriage, the driver spoke quietly to the big mare, and they began to move down the long, curving drive. We lingered to enjoy a few last moments in the tranquil park and Janet continued to wave good-bye and call "Thank you" until they disappeared around a bend and out of sight.

The End